Koichi Takada Architects

Naturalizing Architecture

Koichi Takada Architects

Naturalizing Architecture

Philip Jodidio

New York · Paris · London · Milan

Architecture Is Nature

Béatrice Grenier

At Ryoan-ji Temple in Kyoto, one enters a pavilion from which to contemplate the garden. There, the gaze is led to intricate rock formations delicately placed atop a carefully manicured and ordered multitude of light-gray pebbles. In the background, beyond the outlined plot of the garden, the foliage of lush trees captures the colors of the seasons. Rocks stand as the symbolic representation of mountains in a landscape; the viewing pavilion becomes the evocation of architecture, all coexisting within one scene: the Japanese garden is a microcosm of the world.

The philosophy embedded in the art of the Japanese garden offers an approach whereby both nature and architecture find balance in an entwined cohesion; it is the interconnection and interdependence of constructed elements and natural life surrounding it that render the whole beautiful and meaningful. Nothing exists in isolation: the man-made is but one element of the landscape, yet is central; indeed, it is in the garden where it is possible to understand that the original "technology"—the pavilion—which allows humans to exist within nature, is architecture.

Koichi Takada's architecture today acknowledges what the 15th-century Zen tradition had expressed in aesthetic terms—that there is no possible division between city and nature, landscape and architecture. Each of the architect's buildings is a speculation on how nature might be expressed, in its most modern form, as a complete symbiosis with architecture.

In more recent architectural history, the competition to design La Villette park in Paris was one of the most significant projects in terms of forging a new reflection in architecture and its relationship with landscape. The winning entry, designed by Bernard Tschumi (1983–90), reversed the role of nature in the city, bringing the latter's density, congestion, and richness to the park. Equally significant for the development of urbanism and architecture was the influence of the second-prize entry submitted by Rem Koolhaas. The unbuilt proposal explored the juxtaposition between various park programs—parallel strips of landscape with irreconcilable contents—evoking the adjacent floors of New York skyscrapers lying flat.

While both projects predicted a new relationship that needed to be elaborated between the "park" and "the city" in relation to the notion of "urbanity" and "wilderness," their influence failed to resolve this persisting binary relationship. Even though architectural culture became more conscious of landscape and its role for

The Solar Trees Marketplace (Shanghai, China) reimagines the forest as architecture, inviting people to gather beneath its canopy.

the contemporary city, a dualism long-standing in Western culture has often maintained the idea of landscape as being separate from nature: the former a stylized expression of culture, while the latter an "unknowable" territory.

Koichi Takada's projects propose new principles of mutuality and inclusion between nature, architecture, and culture. The architect's approach is that of a planetary sampling: informed by the essence of nature itself, inasmuch as it takes inspiration from the boundlessness of hybridity of every locality in which he builds. A market as an "architectural forest," a residential high-rise that draws its form from a Moreton Bay fig tree, or from shapes inspired by the Watagan Mountains, invite us to contemplate how the oldest "technology" that has made it possible for man to live in nature might be put to use in defining nature's future, and, in so doing formulate a new culture in which architecture is itself nature.

Ryoan-ji Zen Garden (Kyoto, Japan) captures the essence of the natural world through its composition.

Nature Renewed Koichi Takada

Philip Jodidio

Nature in its many forms and expressions lies at the heart of architecture. From the caves of the earliest human dwellings to the splendor of the Corinthian columns that first appeared in Greece about 400 years before Christ, nature is inevitably the touchstone and the inspiration of the built world. Nature suffuses the lofty vaulted spaces of Gothic cathedrals, allowing only light filtered by stained glass to enter, echoing the most ancient of forests. So many architects, in the image of Antoni Gaudí (1852–1926) or Frank Lloyd Wright (1867–1959), have sought to somehow integrate their work into the natural world, forming an organic connection with what is and what will continue to be. Wright used aesthetics (forms) and materials to create an "organic" architecture, and his concept of the organic was perhaps more personal and subjective than inevitable and fundamental, precisely because it was in good part a matter of appearances. Where seminal figures like Wright and Gaudí sought to design forms that were at once new and still intimately connected to the earth, more recent architecture seems to have bowed low to the sirens of profit and soulless repetition. This trend has been empowered by computerized tools that ease the way to lowering costs and increasing rapidity.

Because the presence of nature has not been deemed "cost-effective" in many circles, modern (and especially contemporary) architecture has broken more and more with its ancient traditions, whatever the discourse of the moment might affirm to the contrary. Urbanization on a global scale has also played a role in the emergence of endless architectural forms rendered distinct only by their kinks and curves, distinguished by their overweening capacity to remove users and residents from the real, natural world. Some of these spaces and places are being created at breakneck speed in parts of the world that are hardly fit for human habitation. Dubai reached 50.7°C on July 8, 2024, while Phoenix, Arizona, registered 70 days in 2024 when temperature surpassed 43°C. Cities in such places are of course exposed to the rigors of climate change, but in terms of ecological responsibility, were they ever appropriate locations for large population centers?

Cosmetic or Cosmic?

The Dutch architect Rem Koolhaas has written convincingly of what has been coined the "death of architecture," or, as he more specifically puts it, the rise of "junkspace." In a 2002 diatribe under that name, he wrote that contemporary junkspace is "seemingly

Park Güell, Antoni Gaudí (Barcelona, Spain, 1900).

Fallingwater, Frank Lloyd Wright (Mill Run, Pennsylvania, USA, 1937).

an apotheosis, spatially grandiose, the effect of its richness is a terminal hollowness, a vicious parody of ambition, that systematically erodes the credibility of building, possibly forever..." In typically brutal fashion he concludes: "The cosmetic is the new cosmic." The shopping centers, hotels, and convention centers of much of the world were firmly in his sights, but his thesis was that junkspace has already become the dominant product of contemporary architecture.

And yet the call of nature remains, if mostly because architecture (or rather construction) has been proven to be one of the most significant sources of pollution and greenhouse gases on the beleaguered planet. The return to nature thus emerges less from lofty philosophical and aesthetic goals than it does from the pressing catastrophe of climate change. Here, too, technological solutions have come to the fore, offering miraculous decreases in carbon footprints, shielding glass buildings from their nemesis of solar gain (maybe three panes and a whiff of argon will do it). Interesting, though, that "renewable" resources such as timber have gained in popularity while the star of concrete has dimmed. Statistics show that concrete contributes four times more to global carbon emissions than the entire aviation industry.[1]

Respecting nature in a formal way might be one description of Frank Lloyd Wright's "organic" designs like Fallingwater (Mill Run, Pennsylvania, 1937), which perched reinforced-concrete slabs over a stream. The appreciation of the negative impact on the environment of concrete is, of course, a much more recent development, but other examples of architecture that seeks to blend into the natural order abound. Shall we dare to cite Norman Foster's Gherkin in London (30 St Mary Axe, 2003)? Actually, the example of Foster opens the discussion to another approach to nature, one of calling on its own properties to reduce energy usage and thus increase sustainability. The profile of the Gherkin creates external pressure differentials that are exploited to drive a unique system of natural ventilation. The pickle may not be everyone's ideal natural form, but a building that uses natural ventilation to "breathe" surely comes closer to the mark.

What Do We Do Next?

Koichi Takada is by any measure one of the rising stars of contemporary architecture and a proponent of a return to nature, but not necessarily through the subjectively driven metaphors favored by Wright. Takada starts instead with figures like Koolhaas, who insisted that the contemporary world has eviscerated architecture to the point of making it meaningless, an elevator ride instead of a genuine experience of space. Indeed, the brutality of Koolhaas gave some the impression that architecture itself was dead, victim of a world made of identical malls, airports, and offices. Takada accepts the negativity espoused by the older Dutch star and says that we are guilty of polluting the planet both in terms of materials

An early concept for a multi-residential project in Taiwan (New Taipei City, 2022) was envisioned as a living façade, composed of 111 architectural "trees." It is designed to serve as a visual reminder of nature's vital role in the future of cities.

and of energy use; we have fabricated cities with no emotion that offer only ephemeral emptiness driven by consumerism. But rather than being resigned to these dramatic failings, he asks, what do we do next? The solution, he says, is to accept the death of architecture as it was and to make buildings that are not only green but as green as they can possibly be, to make them exciting again, and finally to make architecture human again by connecting it to the city and the earth. "We want to facilitate the death of architecture," he says, "to allow nature and the well-being it represents to return. I think it is not as simple and experiential as Koolhaas put it. We need to start from this point to redefine the word architecture in the context of history (the past) as well as the future."

Koichi Takada explains: "The selection of work in this book has a lot to do with trees. A tree becomes a group of trees, and then a forest. The forest can evoke a mountain, and then, perhaps a farm. This is a path of inspiration that we have been looking at. Gaudí said, 'This tree near my workshop; this is my master.'[2] Tadao Ando, whom I admire greatly, has long planted trees. Instead of just creating a beautiful concrete structure, he has found that planting trees is equally important to creating an environment and giving something back to society."

Takada continues: "Kengo Kuma, who wrote the preface to my previous book, has often used wood and other natural materials in his work. For my generation, the use of natural resources has come to be considered a great luxury. There are also fire regulations that make the use of timber complicated in some places. →P. 46 The Solar Trees Marketplace in Shanghai is a good example—it is non-natural in the sense that it uses aluminum for compliance but, nearby, we have planted trees that can reach up to the height of the sixth or seventh story. That means that more than half of the buildings will be beneath a canopy of trees. But that metal comes from what we call 'urban mining,' which is to say recycling materials from demolished buildings. We use industrial materials that come from a greener process if you will. We are not only aiming for a green materiality, or strictly plant-based materials to make architecture, we are also interested in biophilic design. Even if it is artificial, the question is how we can once again create architecture that performs like nature."

Enter Biophilia

The term "biophilia," derived from the Greek for the "love of living things," was popularized by the Harvard biologist E. O. Wilson, who argued that the evolutionary biology of humans has conditioned them to be attracted to the natural world. More specifically, in his book *Biophilia* (1984),[3] he introduced and popularized the hypothesis that "humans possess an innate tendency to seek connections with nature and other forms of life." Going further than the more common "green" approaches to architecture, those who subscribe to this theory argue that buildings need to do more than reduce their carbon profile and make efficient use of resources. Basing their approach on new scientific findings, they posit that architectural environments can and should be beneficial to the residents or workers who use them.[4]

Where architects like Gaudí and Wright had their own takes on the natural world, mostly invested in the representation of forms and materials, other contemporary architects have engaged in speculation about how to bring nature itself closer to the built environment. Koichi Takada is very much aware of the Japanese approach, citing,

Approved mixed-use commercial development (Sydney, Australia, 2024). It was inspired by native eucalypts prevalent in the region.

as he does, architects like Tadao Ando and Kengo Kuma. Another important figure of contemporary Japanese architecture, Toyo Ito, speculated in 2000 about how technology and nature would, in a sense, come together, with the emergence of the electronic world: "Our architecture has traditionally been linked with nature through figuration of movements of vortices occurring in water and air," he wrote. "With contemporary architecture, we must link ourselves with the electronic environment through the figuration of information vortices. The question is how we can integrate the primitive space linked with nature and the virtual space that is linked with the world through the electronic network. Space that integrates these two types of bodies will probably be envisaged as an electronic-biomorphic one. For, just as the figure of a living body represents the loci of movements of air and water, the virtual space will most likely be figured as the loci of human activities in the electron flow."[5]

Façades Made with Plants

One part of the approach of Koichi Takada, as seen in the works in this book, has consisted in multiplying the presence of living plants, as he does, for example, in his Urban Forest (Brisbane, 2030). This is an approach that has been taken by other architects in recent years, including Stefano Boeri in Milan (Bosco Verticale, 2014), or in a more virtual context by the French architect Edouard François (Giverny Oasis, Limassol, Cyprus, 2018). Plants, of course, serve purposes that are more than aesthetic, although greenery is known to have a calming effect. Plants filter the sunlight, the wind, and the air; they harbor various life forms, including insects that have usually been absent in the modern urban environment. Takada's exploration of the world of trees and

→ P. 82

Koichi Takada Architects' Sydney studio model room.

plants can be more specifically seen here, as he points out in the Solar Trees Marketplace (Shanghai, 2023) where a structure in the form of a canopy of trees is accompanied by 50 native evergreen camphor trees (*Cinnamomum camphora*) that will partially envelope the building while also helping to improve air quality. Takada recalls that photos of the site taken as recently as 1984 show that it was entirely forested. "By 1994," states the architect, "there are the beginnings of urbanization. By 2000, it's mostly gone, and 10 years ago, it was completely gone. So what we did was to bring back the forest, but in an artificial form that performs like nature."

→P.46

The Sunflower House (2020), though not yet built, was designed as part of a European Commission study in the context of the European Green Deal. It takes the idea of biophilia to a higher level by moving in harmony with the sun and achieving a "climate positive" status. Koichi Takada often presents his projects along with images of nature. In this case, a field of sunflowers makes the point of the design almost without any need for

→P.100

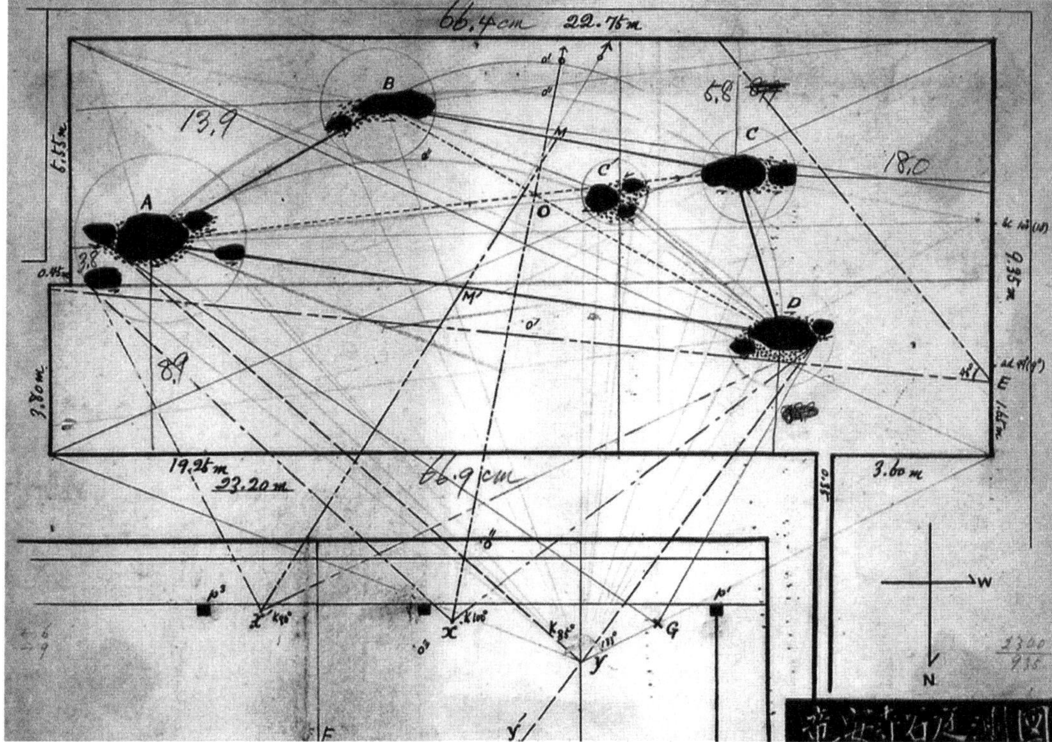

Survey on the Stone Garden of Ryoan-ji Temple, ca. 1938 (Kitawaki, Noboru, Japan).

explicative text. The difference between the designs of Koichi Takada and most other contemporary architects is his commitment to breaking the cycle of junkspace described by Koolhaas, to create buildings that are more and more in harmony with nature. And this harmony is expressed in numerous ways. Takada is not at all adverse to designs that immediately bring to mind natural formations, like the Dahl Al Misfir (Cave of Light) in the center of Qatar which served as an inspiration for his shops in the National Museum of Qatar (2019). Buildings that recall trees and flowers, or that offer remarkable views of coastlines and cities, structures with natural ventilation or operable shades made of aluminum with a woodgrain finish, Takada's repertoire of natural references is both varied and inventive.

The Timber Studio in Tokyo (2021) takes the curving forms of tree rings morphed into three dimensions, while the architect himself refers to Japanese Zen gardens. In describing the forms of the building, he speaks of *enso*, the circles painted with ink in a single stroke by Zen Buddhist monks for centuries, symbolizing emptiness, *oneness*, and the moment of enlightenment. The architect's favorite Zen garden is that of Ryoan-ji in Kyoto. Founded in the mid-15th century, Ryoan-ji adheres to the Rinzai school of Zen Buddhism. Thought to have been created in the late 15th century, the dry garden contains 15 stones. It is impossible to see more than 14 stones from any one vantage point, but it is said that the enlightened can see all 15 stones at once. Though he situates his

→ P. 30

quest very much in the contemporary world and often relates to the context of Australia, where he lives and works, it is apparent that Koichi Takada also makes connections to the art and architecture of Japan. The architect was brought up in Japan and studied in part in Tokyo. For other works like Yugen (Sydney, 2024), Takada refers to another concept of Buddhism, *yūgen*, which is related to the transient nature of beauty. Here, nature enters fully into the design with forms related to the Bird of Paradise flower (*Strelitzia reginae*). Natural stone and woodgrain-finished aluminum are used with moveable screens that provide privacy, shelter from the sun, or conversely open to views of the South Pacific.

→ P. 162

What It Means to Be Green

In his appreciation of what it means to be "green," Koichi Takada finds it relatively easy in his sources to span history, from ancient natural rock formations to the most modern materials. This type of continuity also applies to the delicate question of the history of Australia and its contrast between the very long timescale of the Aboriginal First Nations and the occupation by the English commenced with the arrival in Sydney of a fleet with 700 convicts on board in 1788. "It is a question of moving ourselves to the future even as we include the past," says Takada. "In Australia, it is apparent that the First Nations understanding of the land is based on the natural environment." The architect explains that he has learned to go beyond his own visual sense of nature to

Left Conceptual model of retail interiors for a cultural center in the Middle East, proposing the idea of a "dry garden" in the desert.

Right Concept design for a new cultural destination in Northern Africa enlarges the scale of the dry-garden concept.

learning about what the land has meant to the original peoples of Australia. Significantly the presence of Aboriginal peoples has also been equated with as much as 60,000 years of sustainability that has preserved the land. The challenge for Takada has been one of recognizing the First Nations even in large-scale urban projects. One case in point is Upper House (South Brisbane, 2023). Here, a five-story artwork above the entrance, *Bloodlines Weaving String and Water* (2023) by Judy Watson, a Waanyi Aboriginal multimedia artist, connects the tower to the past and to Indigenous culture. Takada's Trinity Point (Lake Macquarie, 2036) pays a different kind of homage to the Awabakal people, the traditional owners and knowledge holders of the area now called Lake Macquarie. The architect explains: "The current proposal seeks to acknowledge the Awabakal people and the history of the site, providing Access to Country, and incorporating native/indigenous planting throughout the fabric in a meaningful way. Walking Country with elders during a collaborative workshop educated us on the profound Awabakal connection to the local land and waters." Like many other Australians, Takada has taken these very specific historic references into account, much as he frequently references other local (albeit more recent) traditions. His current Sky Gardens (Brisbane, 2030) finds inspiration in local early 20th-century houses called Queenslanders.

→ P. 62

→ P. 210

→ P. 118

Upper House façade artwork entitled *Bloodlines Weaving String and Water* (2023) by Indigenous Australian artist Judy Watson brings a historic narrative to the streetscape within the South Brisbane (Australia) arts precinct.

Opposite left
Native tree species planting initiative undertaken with Aria Property Group (Yuggera Land/Brisbane, Australia).

Opposite right
A Welcome to Country and Smoking Ceremony conducted by a First Nations Australian to begin the habitat restoration project.

The Problem of the Past

Takada's interest for and attachment to the past is as central to his work as his capacity to look forward and to find a specific way onward. He says: "Today, we have to look to something else for inspiration, to create uniqueness or bring back uniqueness, character or personality within homogenous societies. The question is, where do you look? Do you look for the future or do you look toward the past? And then is sustainability the goal or is it the heritage of your society? The problem of the past is how far back we look. Is it as far back as our primitive, prehistoric roots?" Part of Takada's response returns frequently to the country where he lives and works. "In Australia," he says, "we believed we lacked the cultural history of the Europeans, but in fact, when you tap into Indigenous culture, all of a sudden you have this incredible wealth of history. How did they survive in a harsh natural environment all the way up to the urbanization brought on from the West? This is a matter of being able to adapt to changing circumstances, much as we did on a shorter timescale during the Covid pandemic. If we can tap into the uniqueness of the First Nations, we may suddenly be able to create something unique, which can include not only form but materiality, the past and the future."

Aside from Australian history, Koichi Takada has actively sought to integrate elements of nature into his buildings, be it in Brisbane or in the very different environment of Doha, where he designed the shops of the National Museum of Qatar. He says: "We connected with the clients, the consultants, and the builders. We were talking about the theme of nature or in a cultural sense about something that people understand in a basic form. Islam is the culture of the country, formerly rooted here in a nomadic way of life. We seek to create an emotional response with what we design. The natural environment that we reference can have a positive influence on people, looking to the brighter side of the world, and this approach of course connects to sustainability."

The Conundrum of Cost

Koichi Takada's uniqueness springs from many sources, one clearly being the environment and traditions of Australia, but he is certainly not removed from the realities of contemporary architecture. "We still need to build modern buildings in terms of the economy, because otherwise it no longer makes sense. It is either too expensive or too difficult, or it takes too long and has a greater environmental impact. As Norman Foster says, we need to 'do more with less.' There is clearly an emphasis on efficiency in today's world, and architects have to be even more conscious of resources. With an efficient box, you don't find the uniqueness you are looking for; we are being pulled apart in two different directions. Yes, culturally, uniqueness is required, but at the same time, it is necessary to be more efficient, more cost friendly."

How then to make architecture that approaches the natural world more fully while issues such as cost control are ever-present? "In the context of the current environmental crisis, we need to fix this issue in no time. Forms of artificial intervention are necessary to reach a sufficiently high level of performance. We can't just add trees and think that that will solve the problems. We can, as architects, seek to inspire society to shift in a visual and psychological way and to accept more positivity in society. We need the technology; we need to become more and more sophisticated. We can't afford to just integrate nature into our buildings, we need to design architectural forms that are truly inspired by nature.

"Vineyards" is an approved concept for an office building in Sydney's northwest that combines commercial and hotel uses with urban farming. Inspired by the elegance and productivity of vineyards, fertile vines grow vertically up the façade, blending natural beauty with sustainable architecture.

We don't have 200 years to develop this process, it must happen now." And this is where a sense of the profound connection between Aboriginal Australians and the land meets the cutting edge of technology. For Takada, the connection to nature is more profound than offering a clever solution to issues of sustainability—in order for nature to reclaim its place, there has to be a fundamental change in attitude, an understanding that we need the natural world in the sense of E. O. Wilson's definition of biophilia. "Part of the question," says Koichi Takada, "is how to make people themselves reconnect with nature. This can be done through appearance and technology to some extent, but it is also a matter of creating a sense of well-being. The wellness facilities that we try to integrate into our work have a goal, that of maintaining health and sanity in a modern urban environment. In fact, that's where we see opportunities. We see this kind of challenge as a great opportunity to create something unique."

Synthetic Thinking

Where many architects seek to elevate the discussion so that it becomes apparent that their work is a form of art, an almost ethereal creation of the divine spheres, Takada comes back again and again to questions that concern him personally. When he talks about "uniqueness" he is, of course, evoking his architecture, or that of creative architects in general, but he is also touching on questions of personality and life. "There is always so much pressure," he says, "social media, Instagram, you always have to keep yourself relevant. You always have to launch yourself into something. I suppose diversity is the key word. When you try to create your own signature, you hit the walls. When you want to be

National Museum of Qatar Gift Shop (2019), inspired by the Dahl Al Misfir, or Cave of Light (Doha, Qatar).

different, you are asked to conform. It is necessary to remain positive." Positivity is not the most common catchword in contemporary architecture, but it can be seen as the rooted essence of building. Takada demonstrates another quality that seems exceedingly rare amongst contemporary architects, that of a capacity for synthetic reasoning. His idea of returning architecture to nature is one that brings together many different strands of thought, from actual plants lining façades to the beneficial impact of air and light, natural ventilation. He differs from some who would build only in wood because wood is natural—he hungrily employs woodgrained aluminum where actual timber is harder to find and to use over time. He seeks to integrate the artificial and the natural in forms of order that nature provides. Sustainability and well-being are inextricably linked, and both return to the root of positivity.

Bring It Back to Life

Despite living in Australia, Koichi Takada makes frequent reference to his Japanese heritage and to ideas that cross over disciplines and materials much as he does in his architecture. If the word *yūgen*, the name of one of his projects, evokes a sense of beauty that is deeper than words, so too the Japanese tradition of forest bathing, known as *shinrin-yoku*, where one spends time in nature to rejuvenate the spirit. "What we try to achieve is architecture that blurs the lines and pushes the boundaries of nature and design. We of course come up against resistance, but believe that

Retail master plan (2024), designed to prioritize recreation and pedestrians within a dense commercial business district in China. The concept creates an immersive parkland experience ideal for brand activations.

creativity can triumph." What he does achieve is the very sense of positivity that he identifies as a key to the future. He identifies the real issues of modern architecture, from its sameness to its environmental irresponsibility, and he proposes buildings with a sense of emotion and an intrinsically linked desire to return to nature. They may bring to mind a sunlit cave in the desert, a great tree or a turning sunflower; they may breathe in and out like a living organism; they may take on the hues and textures of the earth. With each step, with each new design, they are imagined by Koichi Takada as an effort to approach the living, the natural, the world as it was and continues to be. This is not a quest to return to an ideal past, an Arcadian impulse, but, instead, the result of an openness of the spirit that can accept both the Aboriginal past and the possibility of creating unique and responsible architecture for the future. Ultimately, Takada's work constitutes a response to the condemnation of contemporary junkspace by Rem Koolhaas, by striving to reconnect to nature, to create works that are unique; to infuse architecture with emotion and a sense of humanity, to bring it back to life.

The quotes from Koichi Takada in this text are excerpted from conversations with the author that occurred in London (June 28, 2023) and via Zoom (January 31, 2025). This is the second book by the author on the work of Koichi Takada; the first was *Koichi Takada: Architecture, Nature and Design*, Rizzoli International, New York, 2021.

1 "What is the Carbon Footprint of Concrete," *Greenly*, January 24, 2024. → greenly.earth/en-us/blog/ecology-news/what-is-the-carbon-footprint-of-concrete (accessed February 10, 2025).
2 Josep Gordi Serrat, "El paper dels arbres en l'evolució urbana de Barcelona (1050–1992)," *Treballs de la Societat Catalana de Geografia*, no. 90, December 2020, p. 32.
3 Edward O. Wilson, *Biophilia*, Harvard University Press, Cambridge, 1984.
4 Richard Schiffman, "A Greener, More Healthful Place to Work," *The New York Times*, January 11, 2018. → nytimes.com/2018/01/11/well/a-greener-more-healthful-place-to-work.html (accessed May 5, 2024).
5 Toyo Ito in *On Line, Less Aesthetics, More Ethics*, Doriana Mandrelli (ed.), 7th International Architecture Exhibition, La Biennale di Venezia, Marsilio, Venice, 2000.

Timber Studio 2017–21

Shibuya
Tokyo, Japan

Site area 740 m²
Floor area 1,785 m²

Koichi Takada designed the Timber Studio in Tokyo as a creative hub for a well-known international technology sector client. Shibuya is a central ward in the Japanese capital that is characterized by an architectural and urban environment that some might find chaotic, but which is, in fact, quite typical of Japanese metropolitan areas. The building, set just one kilometer from the famous Shibuya Crossing, the world's busiest crosswalk, has rectangular edges that are willfully contrasted with a "carved-out hollow" that was inspired by the *enso*, the freehand circles drawn by Zen Buddhist monks. Another reference in this hollowed form is the logo of the original client, but that connection was rendered so abstract by the architect that the building today is free of any specific commercial allusion. "We designed an abstract space for creatives to recharge and take inspiration," he concludes. Within the building, a spiral void and staircase connects the three levels. This volume is intended, as the architect explains, to foster casual or incidental interaction between the creative people who were to work in the building. According to Takada: "We brought the calming warmth of natural materials and organic lines into the design by wrapping the façade with horizontal woodgrain louvers. These louvers curve and flow into the building through the shape of a large abstract void." He has also likened the 282 layers of horizontal wood-like louvers to a cave formed by the process of wind and rain, or to the annual growth rings of trees. The dramatic, curving, wood-like forms of the building do recall the real wood used in the giftshops he created in the National Museum of Qatar (Doha, 2019, Jean Nouvel). The building was designed with great care concerning issues of light and sound because recording studios were part of the original scheme. In the Covid-19 environment that upset plans for the 2020 Summer Olympic Games in Tokyo, delaying the event by a year, the client for the Timber Studio never moved into the building. In an interesting interpretation of this result, Koichi Takada likens the Timber Studio to a Zen garden, "an architectural Zen garden, to be seen and not used." "Interaction," he says, "is only in the mind," likening dry Buddhist gardens to "a blank canvas." The best-known example of the "dry landscape" garden (枯山水, *karesansui*) is that of the Zen temple of Ryoan-ji in Kyoto (second half of the 15th century), with its 15 irregular stones placed in a raked field of gravel.

Timber Studio is inspired by the way nature reveals the course of time. Growth rings in timber are expressed in the design, while the creative studio represents the idea of progress and movement.

Timber Studio's organic form evokes a sense of wonder in the urban context. It invites creators to exchange ideas and contribute to a dynamic energy of collaboration.

RISING STUDIO
RISING
PRODUCTION

The white spiral staircase creates a flow throughout the studio and encourages social interaction with pocket spaces in which to pause.

A balcony within the void becomes a lens that brings the Tokyo landscape into focus.

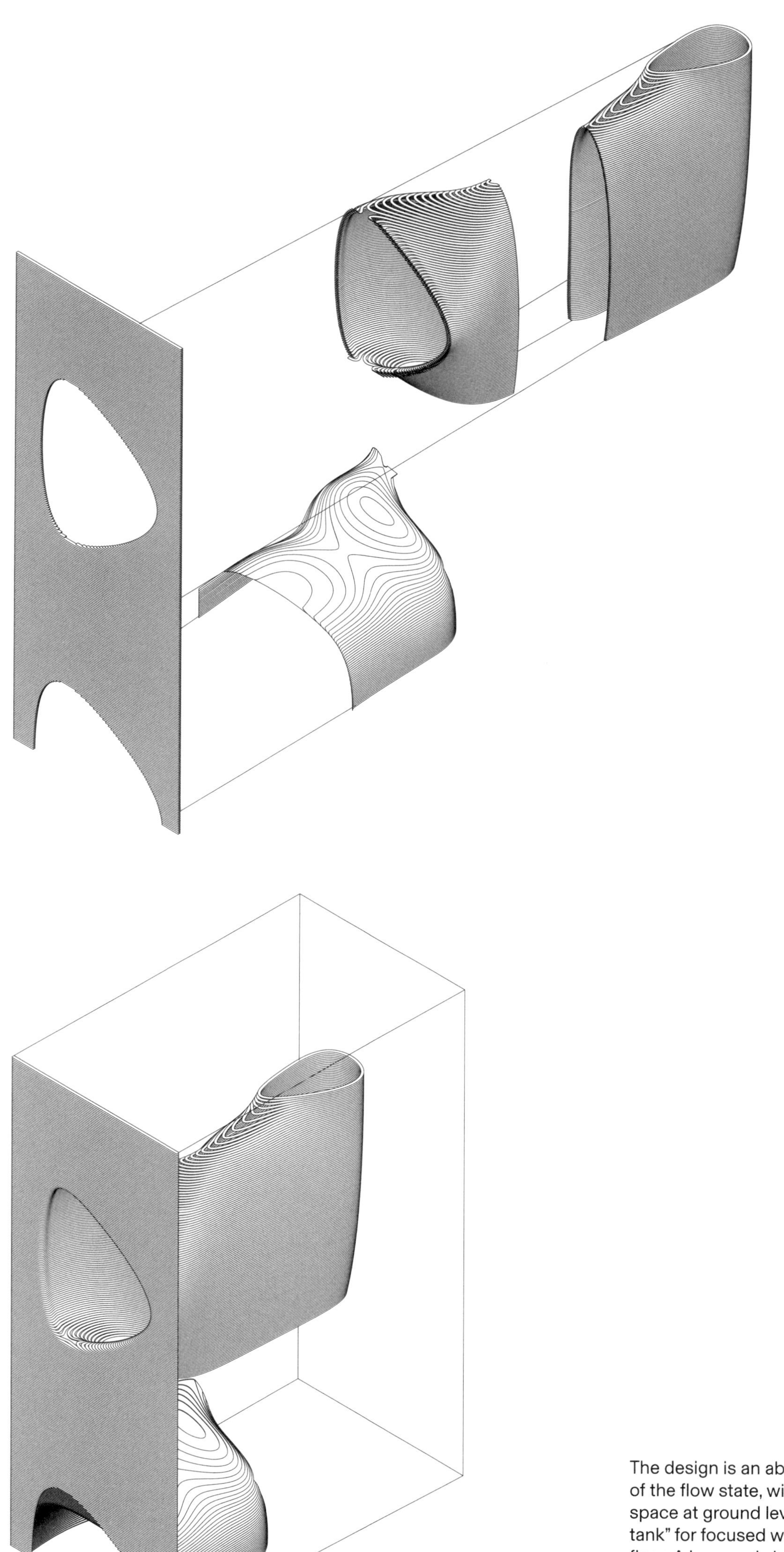

The design is an abstraction of the flow state, with a public event space at ground level and a "think tank" for focused work on the first floor. A louvered shell, modeled and constructed using advanced 3D technology, envelops the building and continues into the interior.

Solar Trees Marketplace

2020–23

Shanghai, China

Site area	3,770 m²
Floor area	3,450 m²

Early in the process of work on this project, the architect learned that the site, 20 kilometers southwest of Shanghai, had been covered with trees as recently as 1984. As a result, he says: "Our design seeks to start conversations around what can be achieved through design and create a living, breathing environment that inspires, nurtures, and adapts to the needs of both residents and the community." He imagined an "architectural forest" made up of 32 tree-like, organically inspired forms intended as a flexible retail space and a "symbol of a future that returns nature to our cities." This is the first phase of a larger development to be designed by Takada which is intended as an immersive sales and display area and a gateway serving the future complex, to include no less than 48 residential buildings and four public structures for a total site area of 180,000 square meters. Once the overall project takes form, the Solar Trees Marketplace will, indeed, become a market area with modular stands like those used in more traditional market buildings, illustrating the built-in flexibility of the concept. The structure emphasizes natural ventilation and provides shade from the hot summer sun. The forms of Solar Trees Marketplace are intended to merge with a promenade of 50 native evergreen camphor trees (*Cinnamomum camphora*), which help to improve air quality as well as underlining the biophilic nature of the architectural design. These trees are part of a future green corridor that will mark the planned larger complex. This structure was built with a steel frame, a woodgrain-finished aluminum façade, and solid-oak timber battens used internally, and is intended to make use of translucent solar panels for electricity.

This site in Shanghai (China) was densely forested only a few decades ago. The design aims to restore nature's role in urban life. The form and scale of the Solar Trees Marketplace creates an "architectural forest" of 32 tree structures, reintroducing the restorative qualities of nature and enhancing well-being within the neighborhood.

This narrow site was reclaimed as a gateway to the 180,000-square-meter master plan. Forty-eight residential buildings and four public buildings, also designed by Takada, are under construction and will be served by Solar Trees Marketplace, which will evolve into a local retail hub inspired by traditional Chinese markets.

The architectural canopy was designed to accommodate photovoltaic cells. This vision prompted the client's acquisition of a solar farm, allowing the entire master plan to benefit from a sustained commitment to renewable energy and environmental stewardship.

大型号牌

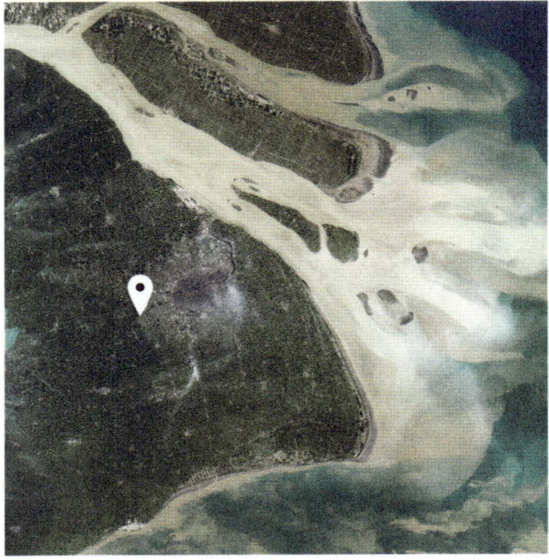
Shanghai, 1984

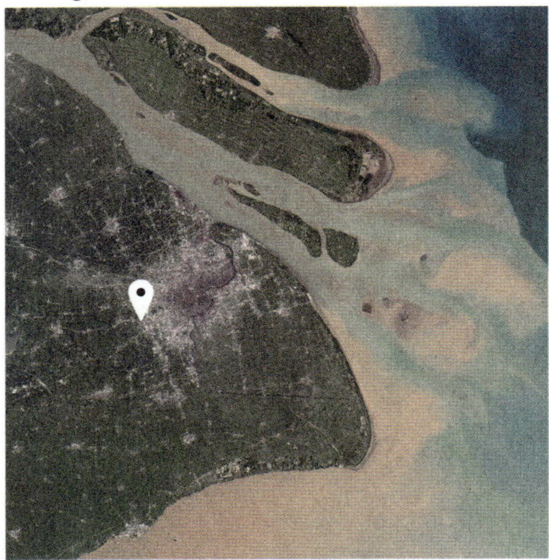
Shanghai, 1994

Shanghai, 2004

Shanghai, 2014

The site in Shanghai (indicated in white) was forested as recently as 1984. The urban sprawl of the past decades has seen nature disappear.

Reversing the loss of nature in urban China, the design introduces a mature tree canopy and deep-soil planters. Pedestrian experience is prioritized, with car access and circulation relocated below ground.

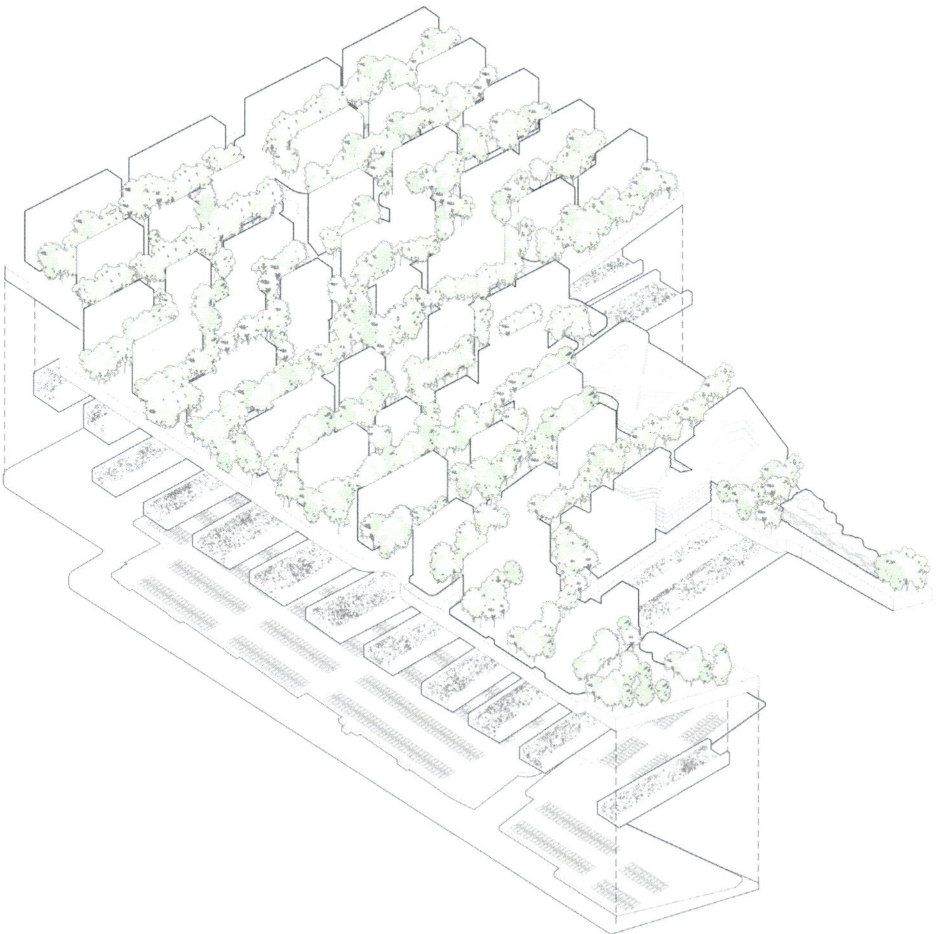

Here, people can live within gardens in the heart of the city. This master plan elevates nature over cars, restoring green spaces for all to enjoy.

Upper House 2018–23

South Brisbane, Australia
Yuggera Land

Site area	1,340 m^2
Floor area	19,700 m^2

Upper House is a 33-story residential tower with 188 apartments that places emphasis on the goals of sustainability and environmental compatibility. Recipient of a 5-star rating from the Green Building Council of Australia, the building was designed to reduce water consumption by 20% over similar structures as well as 100% renewable energy from a 30kW solar system. Landscaping on and around the building provides insulation and reduces the heat-island effect. There are 60 electric vehicle chargers and 242 bicycle spaces in the building. According to Koichi Takada: "The architectural form of Upper House draws inspiration from the Moreton Bay fig (*Ficus macrophylla*), with 'architectural roots' taking us on a journey from our ancient past at its base, up to the future of vertical living. Topped with biodiverse outdoor areas, well-being retreat, and social hub, Upper House addresses what is referred to as connection deficit." The tree-like form of the building, with "roots" that rise from its base reaching its green canopy make it recognizable in the skyline of Brisbane, third largest city of Australia, and capital of Queensland on the east coast. Above the entrance level, a five-story artwork, *Bloodlines Weaving String and Water* (2023) by the the Aboriginal Australian artist Judy Watson, connects the tower to the past and specifically to Indigenous culture. As she describes it, the backlit, perforated-metal sculpture embodies "lines of light [that] crisscross the river and the land. Local routes follow Aboriginal walking tracks. They are the bloodlines that pull us to country and culture." Judy Watson, born in 1959 in Queensland, is a Waanyi Aboriginal multimedia artist. The building has a two-story wellness club and a facility for residents called the Upper Club on two rooftop floors. Altogether there are 1,000 square meters of amenities and no less than 3,544 tropical plants were selected for their compatibility with the local subtropical climate.

The architectural façade of Upper House draws inspiration from the Moreton Bay fig tree. "Architectural roots" meander down the building's façade from a natural timber rooftop pergola to the podium artwork that grounds the design in Australia's rich First Nations history.

PERFORMING ARTS CENTRE

JURASSIC WORLD
MUSEUM
TALLIS

The rooftop pergola functions like the canopy of a Moreton Bay fig tree, diffusing light and providing shelter with tri-dimensional twists and curves. Two timber "nests" (above) on opposite sides of the building accommodate small groups in the open-air cocoons for an aerial view of Brisbane City.

TALLIS

Communal spaces occupy the building's rooftop levels—typically reserved for premium penthouse real estate. These areas are designed to encourage interaction and foster a sense of social community among residents in this high-density, vertical-living environment.

Natural materials dominate the palette inside and become a backdrop to the gallery-like interiors. The ground-floor lobby (above) functions as a public space to support local emerging artists, and 108 original artwork commissions are showcased throughout Upper House.

Upper House supports residents with a well-being-first approach to amenities. Fitness, health, and relaxation offerings span the entire 32nd floor, including hot and cold plunge pools (above) and an infinity pool deck with abundant tropical landscaping and city views (opposite).

HYDRANT
BOOSTER

Bloodlines Weaving String and Water (2023) by Judy Watson. This perforated-metal, backlit artwork enriches the streetscape while thoughtfully screening requisite above-ground, off-street parking.

1

2

3

4

5

6

7

8

9

Wellness Club
1 Yoga Studio
2 Fitness Center
3 Infinity Pool
4 BBQ Area
5 Day Spa
6 Saunas
7 Conversation Circle
8 Hot/Cold Plunge Pool
9 Reflection Pond

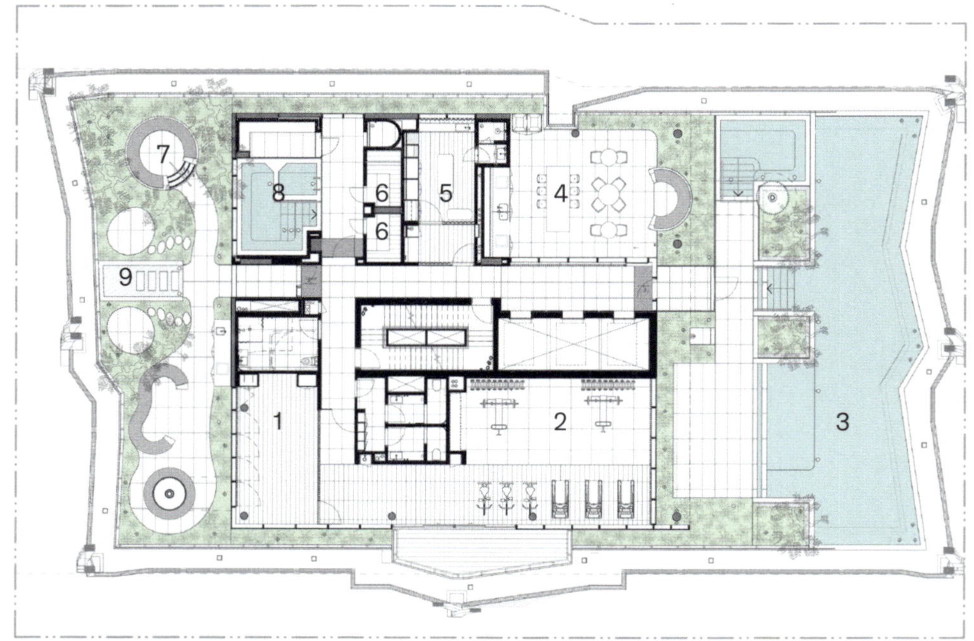

1

2

3

4

5

6

7

8

9

Upper Club
1 Private Dining Room
2 Event Kitchen
3 Wine Cellar
4 Resident Lounge
5 Bird Nest
6 Resident Bar
7 Private Cinema
8 Executive Boardroom
9 Work from Home Facilities

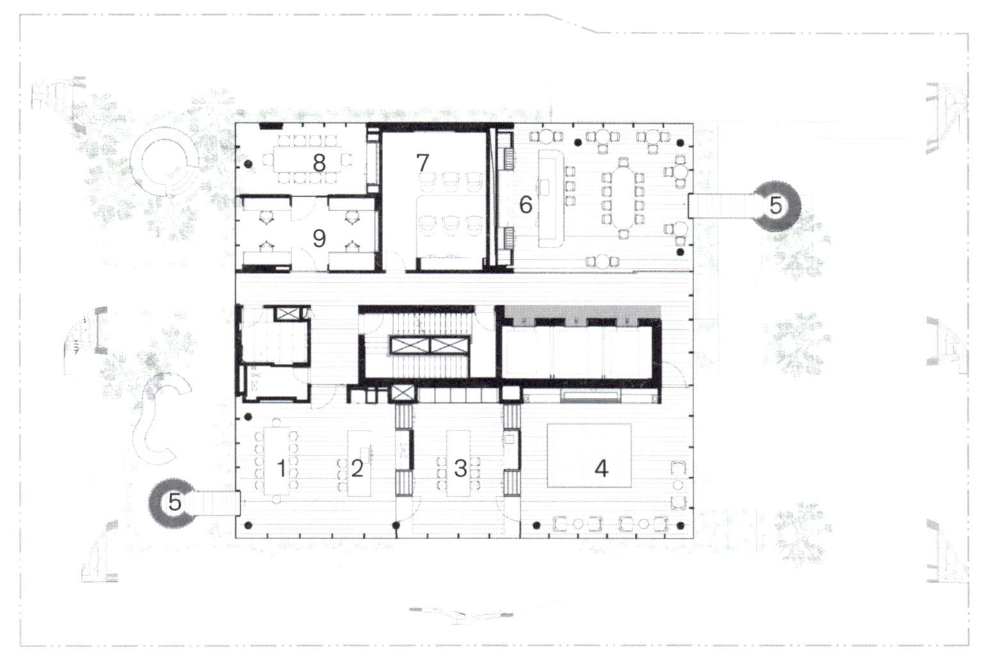

Urban Forest

2020–30

Awarded Approval

Brisbane, Australia
Yuggera Land

Site area 2,784 m²
Floor area 47,000 m²

Urban Forest will be located in South Brisbane. It is a 30-story residential tower with 321 apartments, all with natural cross ventilation. The design features the use of no less than 27,000 plants selected from 251 native species, as well as 827 trees with a total landscaped area of 5,600 square meters. The apartments will have a combination of soil planters that are 500 to 1,100 millimeters deep, allowing for mature trees and plants of varying size, shape, texture, and color to be placed along the façades of the structure. Takada emphasizes the relative significance of this presence, and details that the building will host 10 times more trees than the adjacent Musgrave Park on a site just one-tenth the size, and twice the number of trees in the Brisbane Botanical Gardens. The engagement of the architect in the greening of Brisbane goes beyond the Urban Forest—with his client Aria Property Group, he has been actively participating in tree planting events where native species are added to the habitat corridors of the city.

A two-story rooftop garden includes residential amenities that represent an expansion of the ideas put in place by Takada for his Upper House project. The Urban Forest will have a two-story basketball and squash court, outdoor magnesium baths, outdoor yoga deck, lagoon-style pool, cabanas, and a fire pit, as well as a day spa, executive Work from Home facilities, wine bar, wine cellar, private dining, and fitness center. "The intended feeling," he says, "is like being on holiday. Like forest bathing in the heart of the city." An open public park at ground level with an area of 950 square meters is also part of the project. Koichi Takada's ambition is for this project to be the "world's greenest residential building," with the goal of obtaining a 6-star rating from the Green Building Council of Australia. Intended for buildings that demonstrate "world leadership in environmentally sustainable building practices," this rating is the equivalent of the US Green Building Council's Platinum. Koichi Takada states: "In architecture there has always been this ambition to build taller and taller. We want that outdated metric to be a thing of the past. Now, the greater challenge is to engage in competition over who can achieve the greenest building. That is a contest that excites me... We want to inspire a competitive shift from the tallest buildings to the greenest."

Aside from an almost entirely green façade, which insulates from the rain, sun, and wind, the building has solar panels and rainwater collection. The materials have been selected for their high quality, but also their low maintenance costs. Maximization of natural light and cross ventilation is part of the passive energy strategy of Urban Forest. The project was approved by Brisbane City Council in line with their broader commitment to making the 2032 Olympic Games being held in the city "climate positive." The project is integrated with the South Bank Masterplan, which aims to see "40% of mainland Brisbane returned to natural habitat by 2031." Takada again makes use of images from nature for this tower, lifting it up on tall columns that he likens to tree trunks. This reference also has an echo in local architecture because Queenslander houses, developed beginning in the 1840s and today typical of the suburbs of Brisbane, are lifted up on stumps. This feature encourages aeration and protects against flooding.

Façades with extensive planting are, of course, not entirely new, as can be seen in the Bosco Verticale towers in Milan (Stefano Boeri, 2014), but Takada has taken the idea a step further by integrating passive and active energy saving elements, while also imagining a much more densely planted tower. Jean Nouvel has also experimented on several occasions with planted façades, for example in his Le Nouvel KLCC towers (Kuala Lumpur, Malaysia, 2016), also less densely covered in greenery than Urban Forest. Although other architects such as Vo Trong Nghia in Vietnam have brought plants to their façades, Takada seems to have opened up a new perspective by actively comparing his buildings to trees and other elements of nature—in other words the plants are not just decoration, nor are they a perfunctory bow to sustainability. Nature, the tree in particular, is the message, and perhaps a step forward in the new competition to build still greener buildings.

Urban Forest achieves remarkable ecological diversity and density, inspired by the Daintree Rainforest in Queensland (Australia). The Daintree, estimated to be 180 million years old, is recognized as one of the most universally valuable natural areas on Earth. Urban Forest seeks to give back to the local community and educate more broadly on the natural, scientific, and cultural benefits it achieves.

Urban Forest, colloquially known as Brisbane's "Green Beacon," will return 950 square meters of sheltered park to the public realm by raising the podium up to five stories above ground. An on-site educational facility is designed to service school groups and researchers wanting to learn from the project's ambitions.

Together with Aria Property Group, Koichi Takada Architects contributes to habitat restoration through native tree planting initiatives: 89,311 trees have been planted to date. The trees for Urban Forest are already growing in the region.

Urban Forest will achieve remarkable ecological density (200% site-cover landscaped area), hosting over 827 trees and 27,000 plants, representing 251 native species adapted to Brisbane's subtropical climate.

All apartments are designed to maximize cross ventilation and connect residents to nature. The living façade frames views and enhances air quality, while its seasonal flowering creates a multi-sensory experience.

A living classroom in the heart of the city: this open-ground plane with landscaped gardens serves as a space for hands-on learning, where students and the public can engage with sustainable architecture, urban farming, and innovative technologies for a greener tomorrow.

Forest Floor
1 Residents' Lobby
2 Porte Cochere
3 Concierge
4 Urban Farm
5 Sustainability Center
6 Café
7 Public Parkland & Seating

Elevating wellness with nature: this rooftop sanctuary features expansive green spaces, vertical gardens, and dedicated wellness facilities, such as spas and pools. A serene retreat for residents to unwind, restore, and reconnect with the healing powers of nature.

Canopy Club
1 Lagoon Pool & Cabanas
2 Outdoor Magnesium Baths
3 Barbecues
4 Private Dining
5 Multiuse Room (Podcast/Meeting/Dining)
6 Private Cinema
7 Resident Wine Bar
8 Fire Pit
9 Resident Wine Cellar
10 Resident Café/Lounge
11 Work from Home Facilities
12 Spa Treatment Room
13 Basketball & Squash Court
14 Yoga Deck
15 Fitness Center

Sunflower House 2020

Le Marche, Italy

The European Green Deal, launched by the European Commission and its president Ursula von der Leyen in 2020, was the occasion for several architectural projects to be launched, including Koichi Takada's Sunflower House. In an article published in the *Frankfurter Allgemeine*, Von der Leyen referred back to the founding of the Bauhaus in Germany in 1919, saying the school "literally helped shape the social and economic transition to an industrial society and the 20th century." She called for a constructive 21st-century response to the problems of climate change, pollution, and population increase through the creation of a "new European Bauhaus." She said: "The Green Deal must also be a new cultural project for Europe. [We need] to combine sustainability with good design." On behalf of the European Union, Koichi Takada was asked by Bloomberg Green to design a "dream house symbolizing Europe's green future." His scheme was the first to be revealed to the public subsequent to the initiative of the EU. Going beyond "good" design, he explained: "We drew inspiration for our design from the sunflower, striving to harness the power of the sun. Its roof and each floor rotate on sensors for maximum sun exposure or for optimal performance and user comfort to maximize or minimize heat gain, especially in the extreme heat conditions recently experienced in the Mediterranean climate. Designers and architects talk about drawing inspiration from nature in an aesthetic sense, but we must go much deeper than that," said Takada. "It's not just about making a building look natural, it's about creating positive environmental change in the homes we live in, the neighborhoods we work and play in, and ultimately the planet we are privileged to inhabit."

Imagined as a "climate positive" single-family residence, the Sunflower House was intended to be a fully flexible concept, anywhere from one to three stories in height with three bedrooms on each level. It was proposed that the structures could be grouped in the region of Le Marche in Italy, near the Adriatic Sea, where sunflowers are a favored crop. Sunflowers grow quickly and turn to face the sun exactly as these houses would do, with each floor plate rotating individually around a central "stem" according to solar exposure. Solar panels and sensors would provide efficient energy production, and the rotation of the panels along with the building would allow an estimated 40% gain in their power production. The design provides for panels facing the sun to shade the building's windows, reducing solar gain. In sunny periods the system would generate excess power that could be sold back to the grid or stored in accumulators that Takada has called "battery seeds." Building several Sunflower Houses on a single site would allow mutual shading and other economies of scale that would fully realize the "climate positive" promise of this design.

The idea of a house with rotating elements meant to shield from the sun was present, for example, in the Autonomous House (Los Angeles, 1982–83, unbuilt) imagined by Norman Foster and R. Buckminster Fuller and based on a system of moveable concentric geodesic domes. Fuller's geodesic designs do have parallels in nature in terms of structure, but clearly in 1982 the Autonomous House would not have had the possibility to generate its own electricity for example. Foster currently plans to build a new version of this project on the grounds of Chateau La Coste (Le Puy-Sainte-Réparade, France). Several other rotating solar houses do exist, but none has taken on the biomimetic form suggested by Takada.

Lifted off the ground, the Sunflower Houses would have the advantage of having a minimal impact on biodiversity and protection from potential flood waters. Rainwater capture through the perforated roof perimeter and a system of "earth tube" cooling based on a Roman invention further increase the efficiency and environmental friendliness of the project. Takada's scheme is inspired by both the appearance of sunflowers and their heliotropic behavior, bringing contemporary architecture a step closer to the natural world. Inspired by Von der Leyen's idea of a European Bauhaus, Koichi Takada imagines an entirely new type of architecture where "form follows nature."

Intended to be built in the region of Le Marche (Italy), known for its rolling farmland and yellow fields of sunflowers, Sunflower House draws inspiration from the resilient crop that thrives in the sunshine. The Italian name *girasole* literally means "turn to the sun."

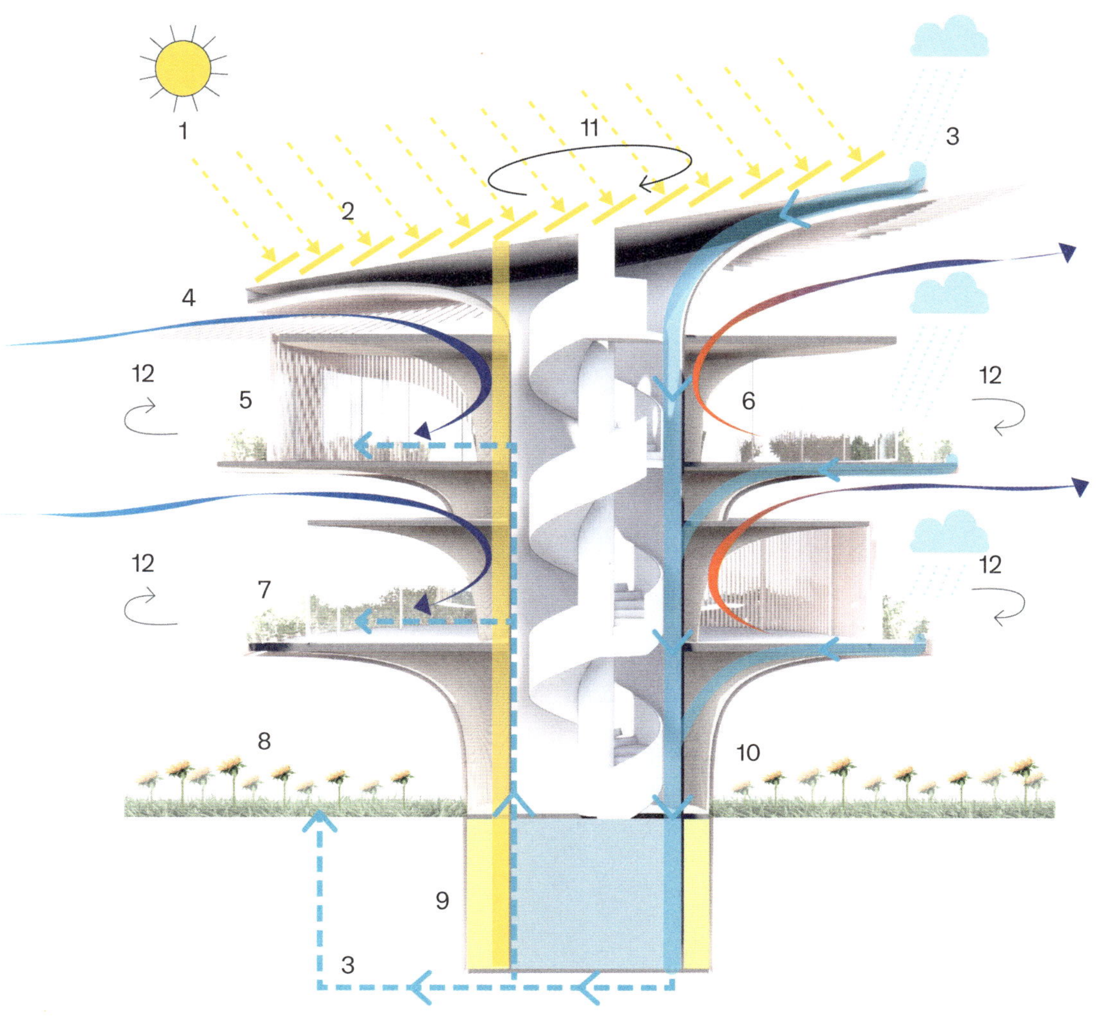

To harness the power of the sun, the roof and each floor of Sunflower House rotate independently using sensors for maximum solar exposure and user comfort. Elevated on a central "stem," the building lightly touches the ground, preserving the surrounding biodiversity.

1 Sunlight
2 PV cells at optimal angles
3 Rainwater collection and reuse
4 Capturing the wind
5 Shading optimization
6 Stack effect
7 Edible gardens
8 Restoring biodiversity
9 Storing energy
10 Elevating the building/Flood mitigation
11 Rotating roof
12 Rotating floorplate

Chifley South 2022

Sydney, Australia
Gadigal Land

Site area	6,438 m²
Floor area	130,349 m²

The idea of labeling and developing the most active business areas in cities has been popular in Australia, with Melbourne, Brisbane, and Sydney all having a CBD, or Central Business District. The CBD of Sydney is, in fact, the city center, sometimes also called Sydney City. About half the businesses in the area are involved in one form of finance or another; it is a main hub for Australia and for the Asia Pacific region. A difficulty with such concentrated areas of office towers occurred with the trend to working from home that has remained significant long after the end of Covid restrictions. "This is a big issue of our time," says Takada. "How do we get people back to the CBD? People are now used to working from home flexibly, indoor or outdoor as they like, changing the mood to suit their preferences. The challenge is to create a working environment, that is, let's say, better than home. We approached this by identifying what's missing from each. What's missing from WFH (Work from Home): social interaction, on-hand support, purpose-designed infrastructure, and tech. What's missing from working in a typical office: fresh air, natural light, being in nature, flexibility/customization of workspace/comfort."

Chifley South Tower is a 37-story structure with a "living façade" featuring seasonal planting, and a degree of "bio-filtration for air quality." A sophisticated trellis system on the façade supports climbing plants that help to achieve the stated improvement in air quality. There are open-air terraces that create a space for social interaction. Connecting to Sydney Harbour and the Botanic Gardens, the design seeks to be a "hybrid of CBD and botanical gardens, taking the best of each for user benefit. The effect is that of working in a garden and being able to reconnect with nature in an environment that is effectively healthier than home." The newer structure adjoins the earlier 53-story Chifley North Tower built in 1992 by the American architects Kohn Pederson Fox (KPF) with Travis McEwen. The two buildings share a common lobby and ground-floor food and beverage outlets. According to Takada, the South building was "designed as a sensitive addition to Chifley North Tower," which "corresponds to the character and proportion of the existing tower." Unlike its older neighbor, the South Tower has a great deal of flexible space, including the floorplates—which can be used to create "social winter gardens" as required. "Where the art deco architecture of Chifley North offers a grounded, formal environment suited to traditional professions," says Koichi Takada, "Chifley South seeks to reimagine the workplace as a vibrant, health-centric workplace of the future." Designed to achieve a 6-star rating in the Green Star system of Australia, the building has an eastern façade that allows openings in recesses to bring fresh air into the communal and social spaces, creating "a naturally ventilated semi-outdoor space."

Connecting as he always does to the history of the places he builds in, Koichi Takada takes his starting point in the history of the Gadigal people, the "traditional owners and knowledge holders" of the place that is now called Sydney. Although the modern development of the Sydney CBD has erased almost all evidence of the Aboriginal inhabitants of the land, the nearby Royal Botanic Garden has themed areas related to the history of native flora and fauna in the area—an inspiration that the Chifley South Tower embraces. The architect explains: "The current proposal seeks to acknowledge the Gadigal people and the history of the site by incorporating native/indigenous planting throughout the built fabric in a meaningful way."

Chifley South reimagines the edge of Sydney's Botanic Gardens, dissolving the line between city and nature. Inspired by the city's natural beauty, this commercial tower brings the park into the workplace, advancing the City of Sydney's Greening Sydney Strategy and redefining what it means to work within a living landscape.

"The invitation to design Chifley South was an opportunity to think deeply about the future of our working lives. We are in an era of great transformation," says Takada. "As architects gifted the opportunity to create a new typology post Covid, the big question remains: How do we bring the people back to our cities?"

MULPHA
GRESHAM

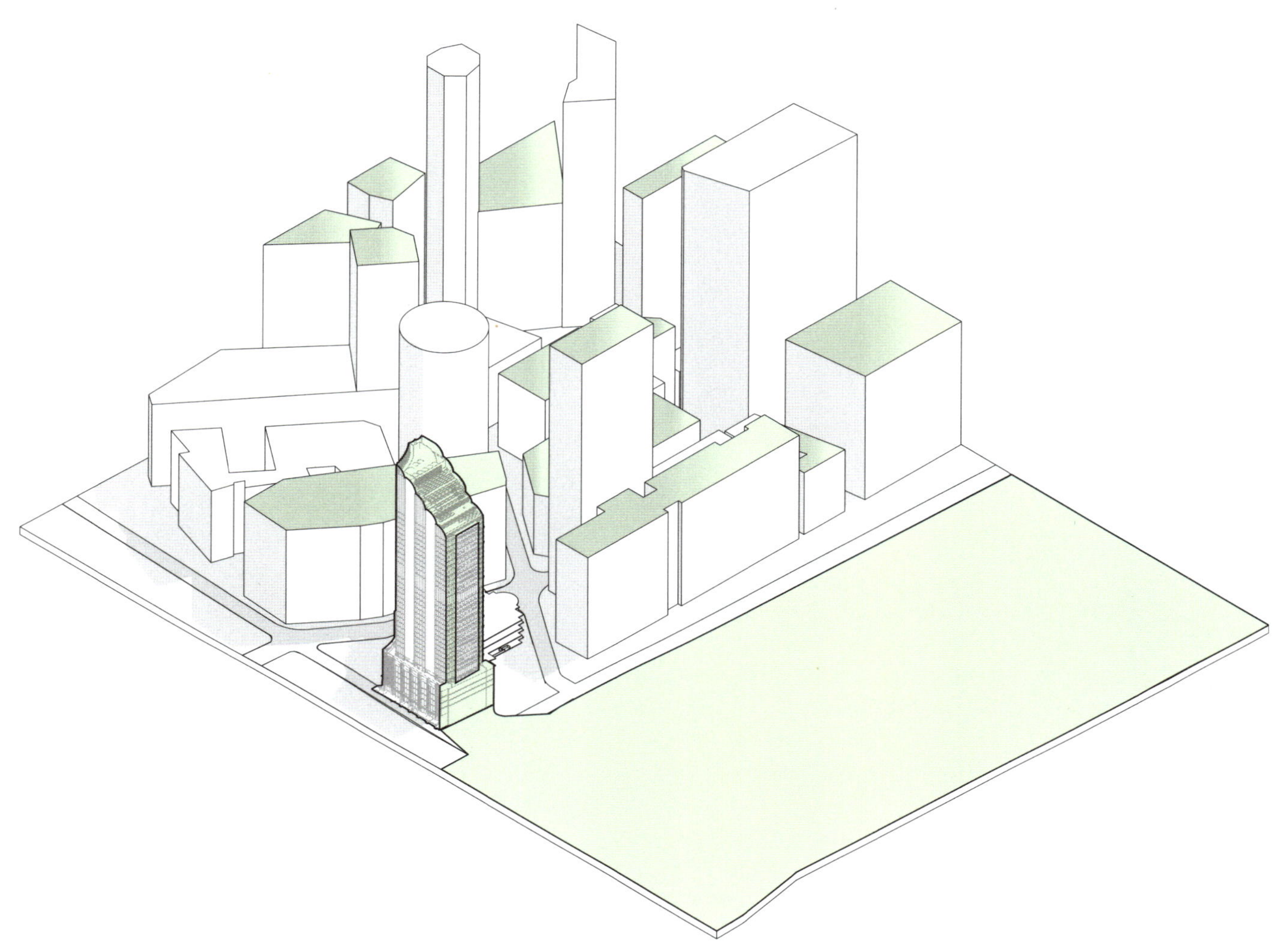

In line with the City of Sydney Greening Sydney Strategy (with a goal to increase tree canopy to 22% by 2030 and 27% by 2050), there is an opportunity to retrofit and re-green urban rooftops and façades.

Sky Gardens

2023–30

Awarded Approval

Brisbane, Australia
Yuggera Land

Site area	2,736 m²
Floor area	71,000 m²

This is a 71-story residential building with 527 apartments located in the Central Business District (CBD) of Brisbane. Takada has imagined five different landscaped recreation areas set on densely planted organically shaped floors that protrude from the basic outline of the building, giving the tower a distinctive profile in the city. Koichi Takada explains: “These protrusions define the five communal resident areas, each offering distinct experiences, from the more intimate garden terrace at low to mid rise, up to the panoramic sky deck. These divisions blur the boundaries between interior and exterior, establishing the building as a prominent icon in Brisbane's skyline while maintaining a strong connection to its natural surroundings.” The amenities of the building include a basketball court, a golf simulator, pools, a wellness area, and a private dining space for residents. High-rise balconies with natural ventilation and selected views of the city's features are inspired here by the well-known Queenslander houses, a kind of archetype of Australian houses. The idea that the balconies of the structure are “breathable” but protected from the wind, in a reinvigorated image of typical Queenslander houses, is original but not at all far-fetched. Queenslanders became popular in the early 20th century and are usually single-story detached houses made of timber with corrugated iron roofs, identifiable also because of their verandas that nearly surround them (but never entirely).

The biodiverse planting of the building's podium features a “waterfall” of living greenery, selected so that some will be in flower at any given time of the year. Targeting a 5-star rating in the Australian Green Star system, the structure will also take art into account with features such as *Paradigm*, a 30.48-meter-high stainless-steel sculpture by the American artist Jon Barlow Hudson. Originally commissioned for World Expo 1988, which took place in Brisbane, *Paradigm* is, according to the artist, “both the DNA molecular structure, which all humans share/world expo, and the *axis mundi*: the world turns round Brisbane during the World Expo.” Significantly, this work was one of the first to be designed with the assistance of a computer and includes a computerized lighting system. Takada further explains: “Art plays a significant role throughout the building. Indigenous artwork and murals on the amenity soffits transform these elements into expressions of identity and belonging. The verticality of the tower is balanced by the podium's horizontal design language, creating a harmonious dialogue between scales.” The high-ceilinged lobby of the building and an “adjacent retail offering” constitute an overture to the street, a sign of conviviality rather than eliciting the idea of a gated community. Brisbane is known to have a housing shortage, a problem addressed by Sky Gardens. In fact, the housing problem is more severe in Queensland than in any other Australian state, and Brisbane, behind Sydney, but ahead of Melbourne, is one of the most expensive cities in the country. “This project not only provides a model for high-density urban living to address Australia's housing shortage,” says Takada, “but also serves as a testament to the potential of architecture to shape and inspire the future of Brisbane.” With Sky Gardens, Koichi Takada takes another step to affirming that there can be an intimate connection between nature and contemporary architecture—here eliciting the image of a tree with the height of the structure and its protruding garden floors with hanging plants that are visible from a distance. Moving away from the stereotypical modern apartment with its identical soulless forms, Takada breathes new life into the city with the presence of nature and references to the history of Brisbane and its region.

Inspired by the way trees support life in various forms, from roots all the way up to the canopy, Sky Gardens relates to its environment with adaptable, responsive architecture. A podium designed for human benefit meets Brisbane City at ground level, while elevated amenity levels segment the tower and support the various needs of the mixed-use typology.

25 MARY

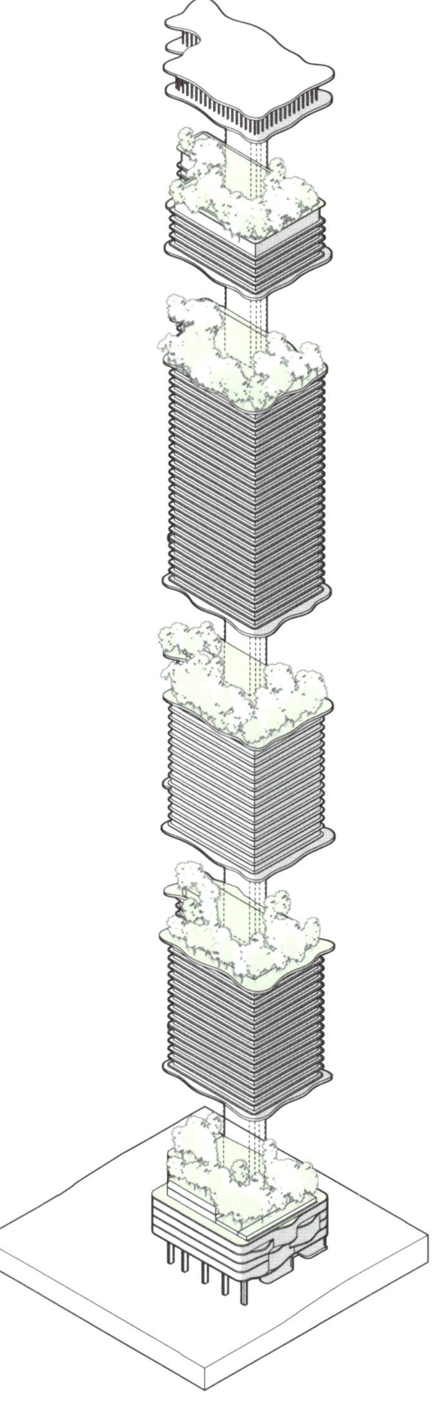

Designed to be future proof, Sky Gardens is a mixed-use tower that allows for various functions. Commercial tenancies, hotel suites, residential apartments, and premium "Sky Homes" are interspersed with five amenity decks, which can be tailored to their specific needs.

Landmark by Lexus 2022–24

Melbourne, Australia
Wurundjeri Land

Floor area 191 m²

This three-story temporary structure was installed in 2019 at the Flemington Racecourse in Melbourne. The 1.27-square-kilometer area is located next to the Maribyrnong River and has been used for horse racing since 1840. It is home to the popular Melbourne Cup and its attendant Carnival which attract nearly 300,000 people each year. The structure is in steel, but a significant part of the design is devoted to the planting of 1,000 native Australian plants on its façade, including edibles such as pepper and lemon myrtle that visitors were encouraged to taste. Takada states: "We are at a time in history when it is crucial to act, to restore the balance. I believe nature holds the answers. And I'm using architecture to start the conversation… Reintroducing trees and plants to man-made environments can reduce inner-city temperatures, increase biodiversity, and reduce our stress levels at the same time." A modular structure allows for the pavilion's façade to be adapted and reused, clearly increasing the sustainability of the design, which received a "carbon neutral certification." The original modular black "box" was designed by the Dutch-born florist, artist, builder, and environmentalist Joost Bakker in 2019 to be used each year. Koichi Takada Architects came on board beginning in 2022 to reimagine the pavilion with an emphasis on organic forms and sustainability, adding curving balconies, awnings, and plants to the originally rectilinear structure. Their modular solution was put in place in 2022, 2023, and 2024. The balconies are a reference to the curving rock forms of the Boroka Lookout in the Grampians National Park, northwest of Melbourne. Interiors of the 2023 pavilion were by the Melbourne-based Fiona Lynch Office.

The temporary pavilion draws inspiration from the resilience and beauty of the Australian landscape. Designed as an immersive experience, the façade holds over 1,000 native plants—a living installation designed for sensorial pleasure, and to emphasize the practice's vision for harmony between urban design and the natural environment.

Guests are encouraged to interact with the façade plantings, which include edible natives such as pepper, saltbush, and lemon myrtle. Interactive culinary moments are curated for guests, with the idea that they would pluck directly from the plantings to activate the senses.

LEXUS

LEXUS

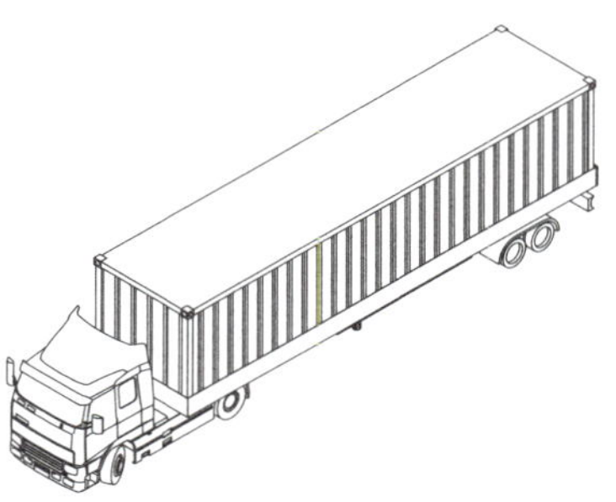

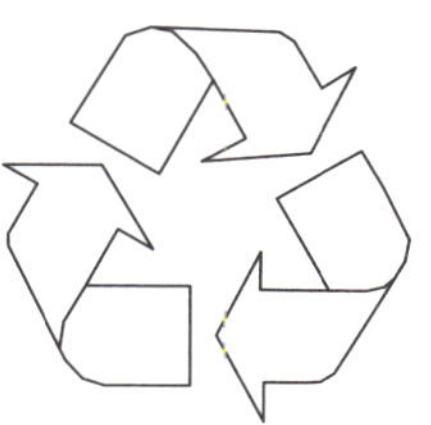

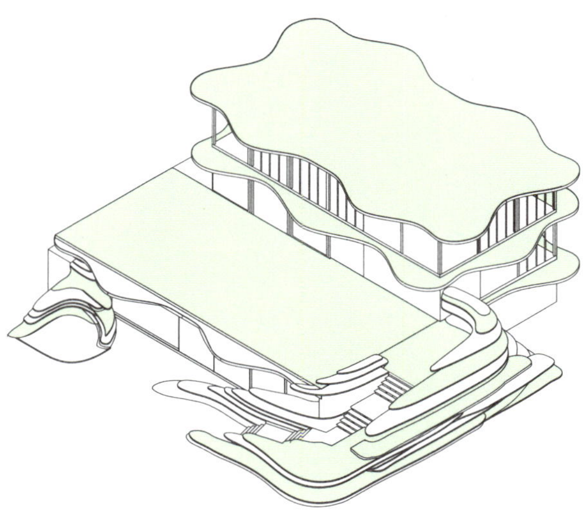

Assembled for the week-long event, and dismantled each year for container storage, Landmark by Lexus continues to reuse the structure and, as a result, was the first pavilion certified as Carbon Neutral there.

Chiswick
Sydney, Australia
Wangal Land

Site area 942 m²
Floor area 563 m²

Chiswick is an inner suburb of Sydney, located about nine kilometers west of the city center. The natural inspiration for the forms of this six-bedroom house, and particularly its protected decks, comes from the sandstone ridges in Sydney Harbour. The residence steps down the sloped site to the water, and the stacked balconies offer wide views of the river. The bedrooms, together with the master suite, are located on the top level, which has a full-width balcony. Because the site running between Fortescue Street and the Parramatta River is long and narrow, the balcony, facing the harbor, is almost as wide as the lot. The Parramatta River is the main tributary of the harbor. An external wall on the northern side of the house provides privacy vis-à-vis a neighboring property, while woodgrain battens and glazing on the south allow winter sun in and provide views out to the bay. Public areas—kitchen, dining, and lounge—are on the ground floor with another living area, wine cellar, fitness space, and sauna on the lowest floor. The property is completed, another step down the slope, by a swimming pool, sundeck, and the boathouse down at the water's edge. The "infinity" design of the pool gives the impression of a direct connection between the terraces and the inside of the living areas with the waters of the river. The double-height entry has a timber façade and a 3.3-meter front door. Staircases—the internal one lit by skylights and a white, spiraling external one connecting the balconies—are prominent elements of the design. Woodgrain-finished aluminum is used for paneling on the southern wall and in the balcony soffits. The color scheme of the house, inspired by neighboring Sydney Harbour, is emphasized by the use of marble, timber, and sandstone. The residence projects a clear but understated image of luxury. The site is constrained but prestigious and the architect makes the most of this unusual configuration.

In Cove, architecture becomes a lens through which the landscape is both framed and celebrated. Its form is inspired by the sandstone ridges of Sydney Harbour's waterline, and the home appears to be carved into a series of fluid, sheltering spaces, as though sculpted by the wind, rain, and waves.

20
18

Cove is a journey that unfolds as you move down the site toward the water. The house follows the steep slope, creating a dramatic double-height entry. Its long, narrow shape brings natural light deep into the interiors through a series of skylights.

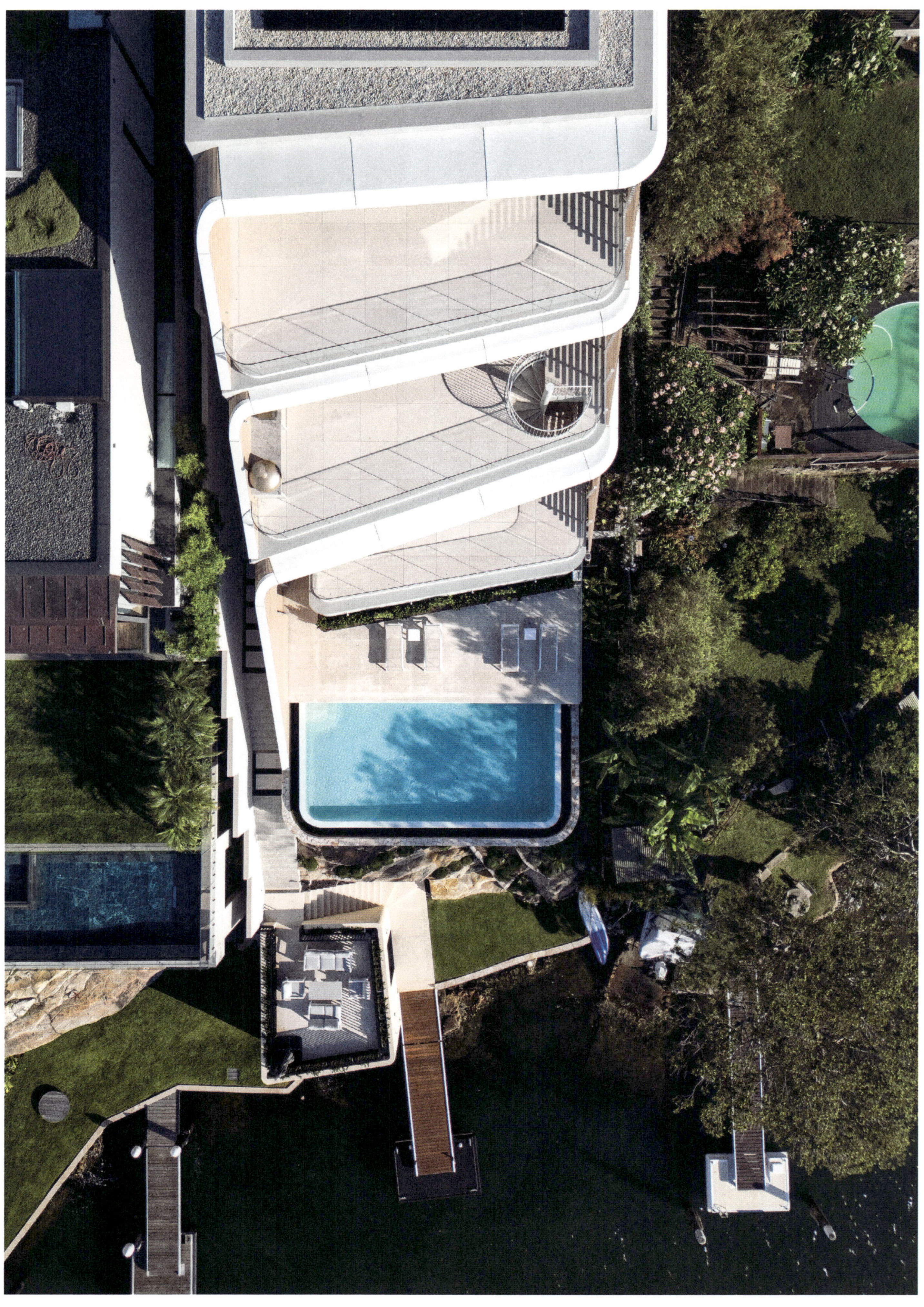

As Cove steps down toward the water, each balcony twists to better frame panoramic views of the harbor, creating a strong connection between architecture and the landscape. A sloping wall offers privacy along the northern edge of the house.

A light-filled stairwell links the private owner's entry with the gallery-like guest entrance. Shifting sunlight from the skylight overhead casts changing shapes and patterns throughout the day. The layering of forms along the steep site creates an unfolding spatial experience.

Tree Apartment 2016–19

Surry Hills
Sydney, Australia
Wangal Land

Site area 312 m²
Floor area 1,282 m²

With his Tree Apartment, Koichi Takada touches on something of a grown-up fantasy, that of living in the trees, somehow suspended between the sky and the earth, closely connected with nature. He refers to it as a "light-filled sanctuary within the urban village." Surry Hills is an "inner" suburb located southeast of Sydney's Central Business District, and five kilometers south of the celebrated Opera House. It is in a high-density urban area but has streets lined with London plane (*Platanus x acerifolia*) trees. As the architect explains: "The design of the building is a response to the trees that typically shade the streets and terraces beneath, opening up a new dialogue above the treetops." The nine-story building has 18 north-facing apartments, and an undulating glass and vertical woodgrain-aluminum-batten façade that "evokes the delicate verticality of a forest," allowing dappled light to filter inside much as it would in a natural setting. This façade creates privacy and security while encouraging natural ventilation. The battens make use of aluminum that absorbs and releases heat gradually, further obviating the need for excessive artificial heating in winter or cooling in summer. Aside from this practical result of the system, the vertical openings of the façade allow for a sense of openness and freedom even in a building that is so close to the center of a major city. For the upper floors, glass balustrades were used to allow for open views over Sydney. On the roof, a pool and lounge provide residents with a 360° panorama of the city skyline. In this shared or social space, the architect refers to the Japanese concept of *shinrin-yoku* (literally forest bathing). Unlike some guiding ideas of Japanese design, *shinrin-yoku* is not ancient, even if it is based on a very specific relation to nature. The term was coined in 1982 when several studies in Japan concluded that bathing in a forest could have therapeutical benefits. The practice (albeit in natural forests) has been encouraged since that date. Materials with natural content such as terrazzo, oak floors, stone, and marble bench tops inlaid with brass were selected for interiors to imbue the spaces with something of the timeless aesthetic implied by the treetop theme. Although it might be argued that some connections to nature can be subjective, Koichi Takada is actively seeking real links between the natural world and the artificial and usually arid world of contemporary architecture. Nor is he sectarian when it comes to interpreting and implementing ideas that are inspired by nature—this woodgrain-batten façade makes use of aluminum rather than implementing a purist definition that would surely have made the building less resistant. Nature has its own ways of changing and renewing; if architecture is to follow in its image, it must find ways to overcome the ravages of time without the benefit of organic growth.

21
the Fabri
Store

The design focuses on creating a sanctuary in the city, offering a retreat from today's fast-paced life. Tree Apartment's façade mimics the verticality of a forest, with slatted screens that filter light like sunlight through a tree canopy.

Each of the 18 north-facing apartments is designed to maximize natural light and ventilation. Featuring floor-to-ceiling glazing and deep balconies, the bathrooms can be completely opened up to allow fresh air to flow through and evoke the sense of bathing among the tree tops.

Beyond its aesthetic appeal, the façade serves functional purposes. It provides privacy and security while facilitating natural ventilation and reducing reliance on artificial heating and cooling.

A communal rooftop lounge area and pool offer 360-degree views of Sydney's skyline and encourage interaction among all residents. Circulation spaces, such as the central stairs, are designed to feel light and open, rather than confined by a solid massing of walls.

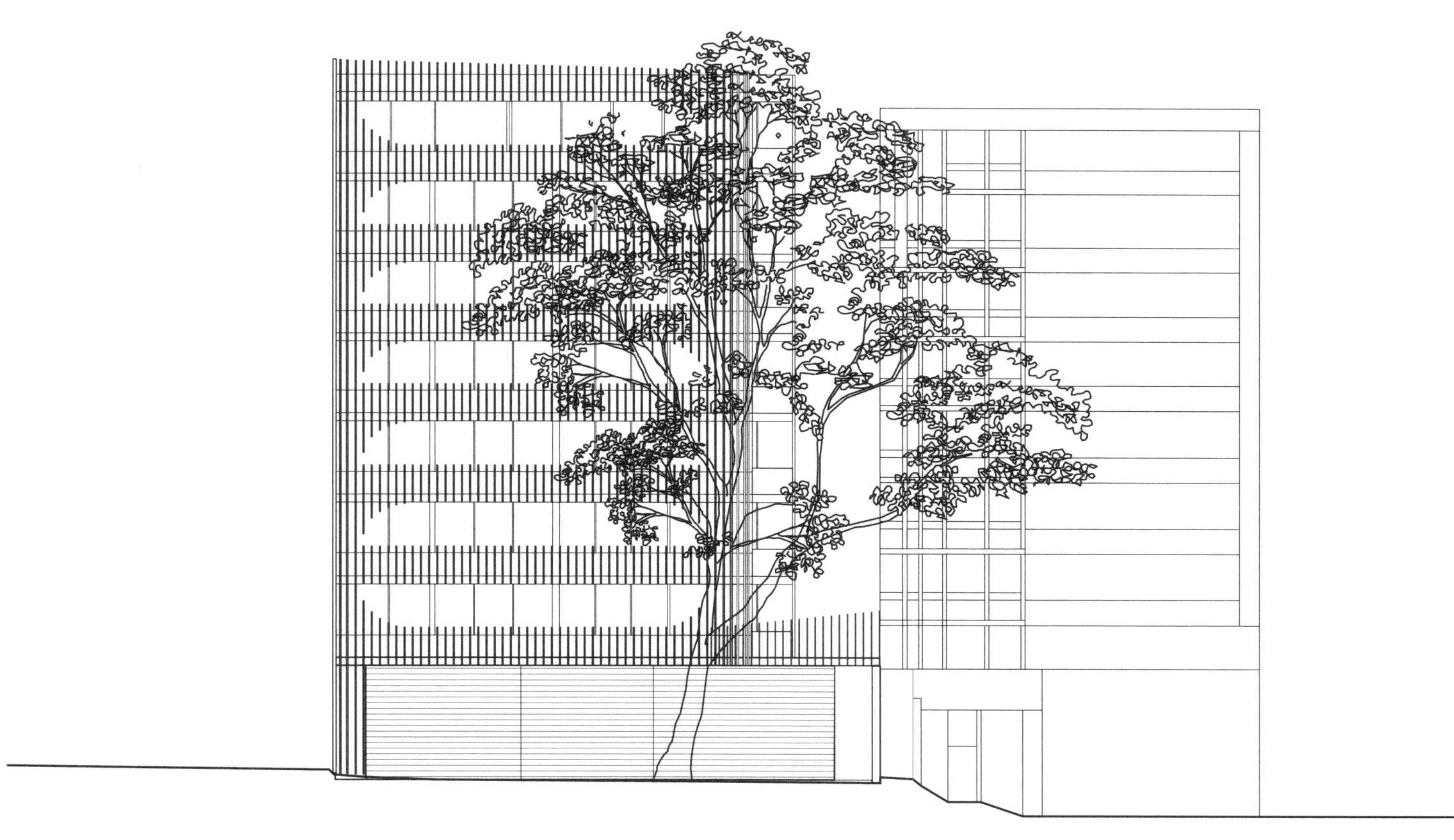

This screened structure emulates the serenity of a tree canopy, with its scale reflecting the surrounding trees. The design allows the architecture to gently recede, placing the emphasis on the established natural landscape.

Vaucluse
Sydney, Australia
Gadigal and Birrabirragal Land

Site area	784 m²
Floor area	793 m²

Yugen is a five-story apartment building with just six apartments located in Vaucluse, an affluent suburb of Sydney, on the South Pacific shore, just eight kilometers east of the Central Business District. A more relaxing proximity is afforded by Bondi Beach to the south and Watsons Bay to the north. Moveable screening allows residents to control sunlight and wind, or discretion as they frame views. Takada was responsible for both the architecture and the interiors of this building. The design refers to the Bird of Paradise flowers (*Strelitzia reginae*) with their extended petals—here compared to the retractable screens and balconies "reminiscent of the flower's bracts." The material palette of the building is related to its natural surroundings, with sandstone cladding "and finishes that reflect the glistening sunlight on the ocean and evoke the coastal landscape." The interiors focus on an ease of transition from indoor to outdoor living with full-height glazing, natural stone surfaces, and vertical woodgrain-finished aluminum screening. Takada, who is of course of Japanese origin, defines the word "yugen" (*yūgen*) as "the way we sense beauty within." As is often the case in Japan, such words have multiple or complex meanings. Often related in Zen Buddhism to the state of emptiness (*mu*), *wabi*, *sabi,* and *yūgen* refer to the emergence (and disappearance) of beauty—with *yūgen* being more focused on the hidden depths of grace and beauty. In all legitimacy, the transience of beauty can be evoked in the context of a work of architecture that is to some extent dependent on the actions and movements of its residents, corresponding in part to climatic conditions. Given its scale and privileged location, Koichi Takada's Yugen may evoke the ambition of attaining an allusive state of grace where architecture once again enters a harmonious relationship with nature. Every aspect of the architecture, says Takada, is intended to provide residents with moments of tranquility and inspiration. The moveable screens "provide privacy and shade while framing views of the iconic Sydney coastline, embodying the delicate balance between openness and seclusion." This adaptability, he continues, is both functional and poetic, reflecting the ever-changing nature of the coastal environment.

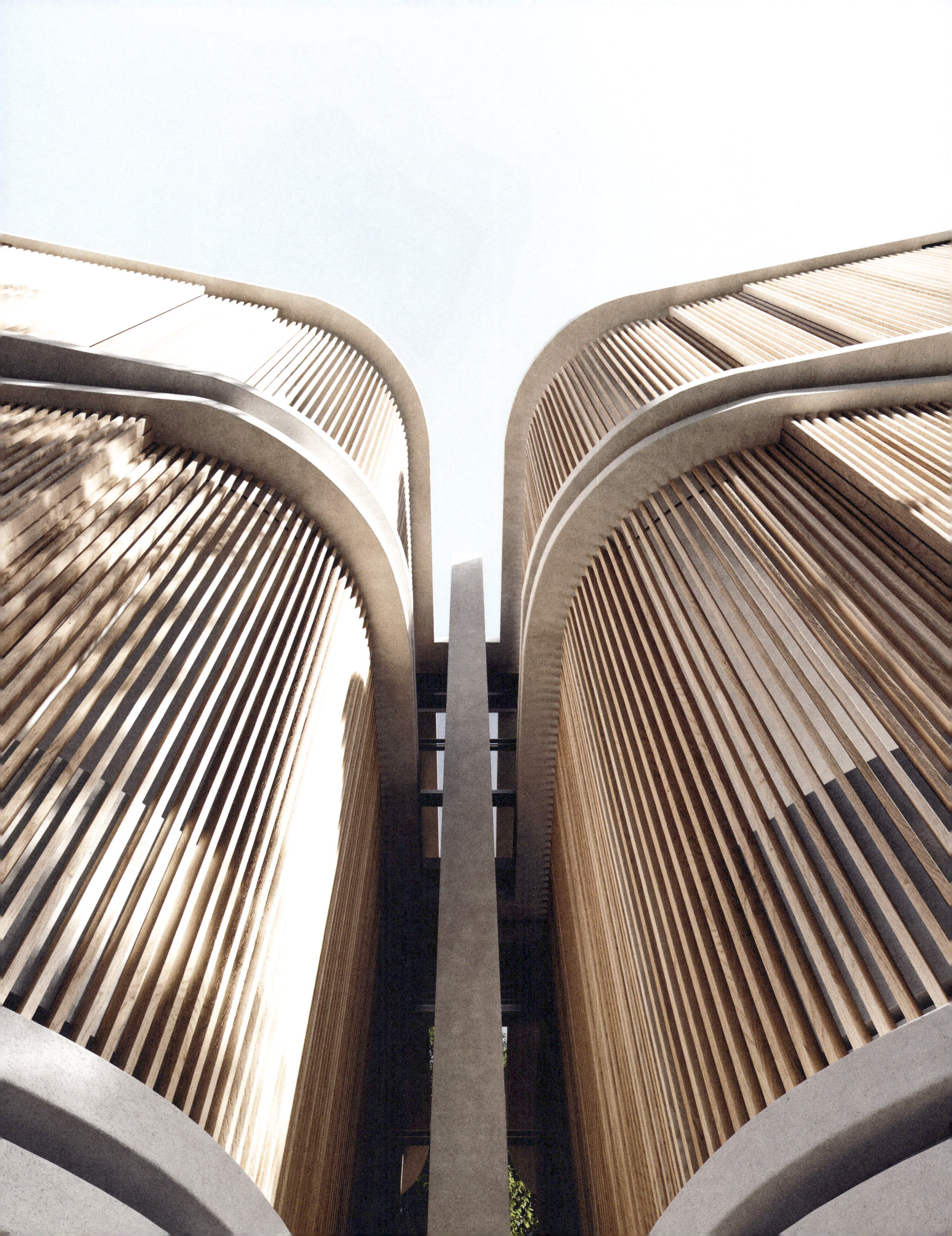

Inspired by the Bird of Paradise flower (*Strelitzia reginae*), Yugen's angles help to direct residents' views. The façade features operable louvers that allow occupants to control their environment for comfort year-round.

Operable doors create indoor-outdoor living spaces reminiscent of an open-air pavilion, with panoramic views of the Pacific Ocean and Tasman Sea. An existing mature fig tree wraps around and shelters the northeastern corner of the boutique complex.

The apartments are designed to take advantage of dual aspects, opening to both the north and the south. The northern side captures warm sunlight and looks out toward the tree canopy, while the southern side is naturally shaded, offering calm views of the water. This orientation means residents can always choose a comfortable spot, to connect with the surrounding landscape.

Yugen's façade is conceived as a dynamic architectural element. Designed to offer residents agency over shading, view lines, and privacy, the operable components create a "living façade."

Palm Frond Retreat 2016–22

Balmoral
Sydney, Australia
Borogegal and Cammeraygal Land

Site area 934 m²
Floor area 558 m²

This home was built on a sloping site above Balmoral Beach in Mosman, a suburb of Sydney, located about eight kilometers northeast of the city center. The architect explains: "Palm Frond Retreat is designed for the family to 'migrate' throughout their home depending on the season and time of day. They can follow the sun or avoid it in the heat of summer." The five-bedroom, three-story house is intentionally focused on views of the water. A centrally located kitchen separates the family areas from spaces for receiving and entertaining. Large, retractable windows permit a direct, open connection between inside and outside. Completing this connection, "materials and hues of the architecture were selected in keeping with nature's palette." Symmetrical linear screening inspired by the effect of palm fronds was chosen to protect privacy, reduce solar gain, and to direct views toward the beach and waterways. South-facing terraces and balconies, like the master suite, make the most of the broad views available from the coveted site, which is near more conservative or "stately" homes. At the northern end of the house, a sheltered terrace is connected to the kitchen and informal living areas. The lower-ground floor has informal spaces at the level of an infinity pool. On the top level of the house, reached via a central, sculptural staircase, bedrooms for the adult children overlook the northern terrace. A study and bathroom are on the areas. The lower-ground floor. Although it is close enough to the city to be considered a full-time home, the location and the design favor a holiday-like feeling.

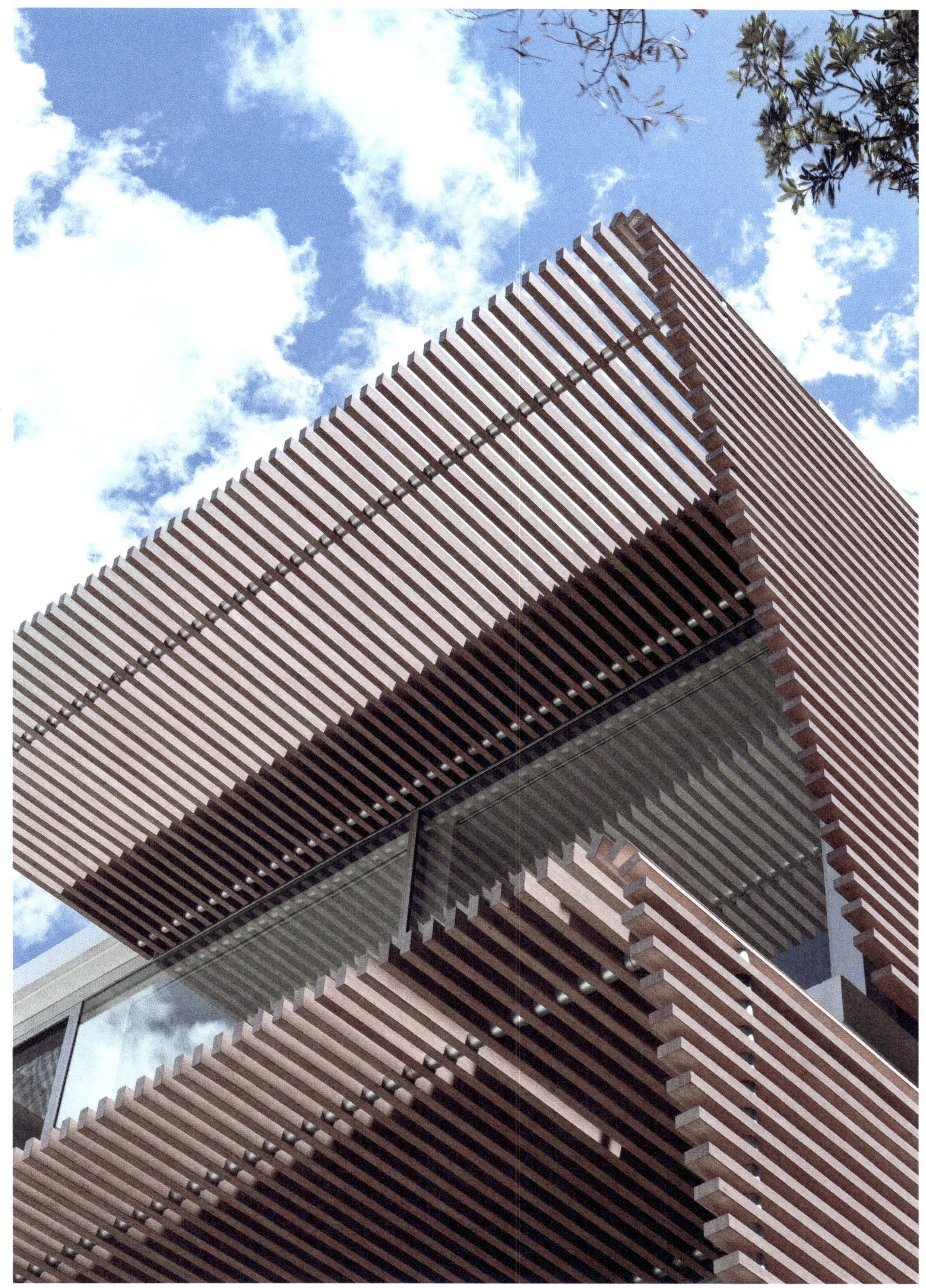

Palm Frond Retreat draws inspiration from the way palm frond leaves overlap to shade and protect the tree's fruit. Applying the same principles, the house uses linear screens to increase privacy, protect glazing against solar heat gain, and direct site lines toward the tree-lined harbor and beaches.

The formal dining area opens directly onto the balcony, creating a seamless indoor-outdoor entertaining space with views over Balmoral Beach. A centrally positioned staircase, with a skylight above, draws natural light into the heart of the home, which is an area often left in shadow.

The entry to the home is through a terraced garden, taking visitors on a journey that connects them with nature as they walk from the street to the front door. Landscape corridors were introduced on both sides of the house and ensure a green outlook from every room.

Norfolk 2019–21

Burleigh Heads
Gold Coast, Australia
Bundjalung Land

Site area 1,012 m²
Floor area 8,510 m²

This 10-story building with 15 apartments is in Burleigh Heads, a suburb south of the city of Gold Coast on the eastern seaboard of Australia. The architect used sliding woodgrain-finished aluminum screens to heighten "the natural softness of the form and provide greater flexibility for each apartment. The design," according to Koichi Takada, "interacts with nature and is very much about creating breathing space for an incomparable beachfront living experience." Views from the building are framed by National Trust-listed Norfolk pines (*Araucaria heterophylla*) which can grow to a height of over 30 meters. Endemic to Norfolk Island, an external territory of Australia located between New Zealand and New Caledonia, these trees have been cultivated near the Gold Coast following their discovery during the second expedition of Captain James Cook (1772–75). Takada explains: "Norfolk's sculptural façade references the inner workings of Norfolk pines, a natural icon in the Gold Coast region. Just as their pinecones protect seeds from bad weather and open when in ideal natural settings, Norfolk's architecture can be adapted to protect residents from the elements or opened to take in the 300 days of subtropical sunshine and stunning natural surroundings." The passive energy design features such elements as offset balcony slabs with tapered edges designed to shade the spaces below. The curved horizontal battens, which form a central spine of the design, serve as sun shading as well as providing privacy while allowing 180° views of the coast from north-facing apartments. The design also provides for natural cross ventilation and ample natural light. Two penthouse apartments have rooftop terraces and private plunge pools, while all residents can benefit from the ground-level sauna, gym, and an outdoor pool. As the architects explain, the material palette of the building, "is informed by the surrounding landscape, the hues and textures of the sand, water, trees, and sky..." Natural timber floors chosen for the apartments connect with the outdoor spaces allowing "life to spill out to generous balconies, blurring the definition between inside and out."

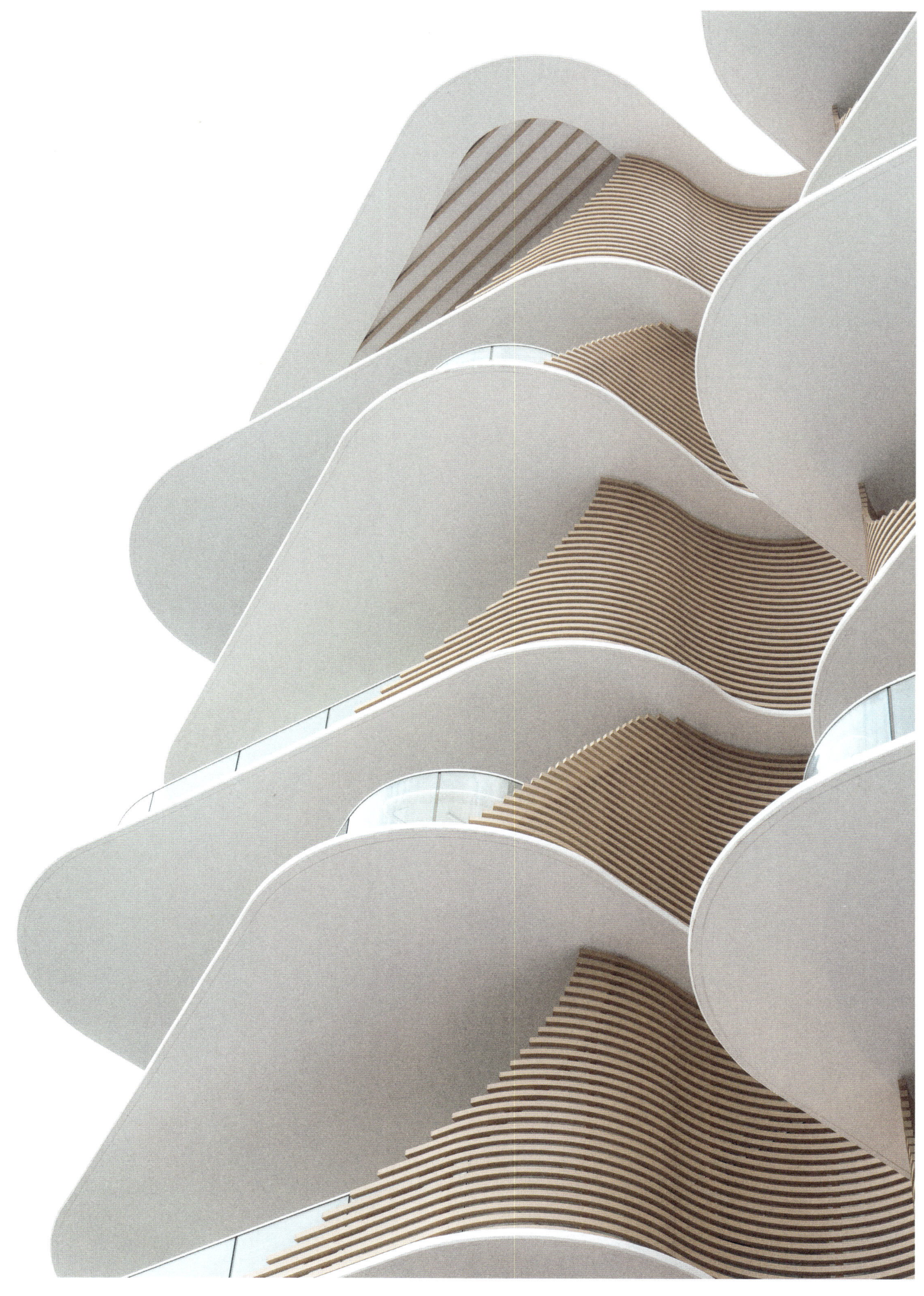

Inspired by the protective form of a Norfolk pine's pinecone, which opens when conditions are perfect, Norfolk is designed to adapt to coastal weather conditions. Mirroring the pinecone's responsive nature, the façade system allows apartments to be opened and closed in response to the subtropical climate.

North-facing apartments offer panoramic views of the coastline. Each residence is thoughtfully designed to maximize cross ventilation and allow ambient natural light to flow deep into the interior. Spacious living areas extend onto generous balconies, with full-height sliding doors and retractable screens for a flexible indoor-outdoor experience.

Burleigh Heads is a revered strip of Australian coastline, currently experiencing a wave of new developments. It was vital that the architecture of Norfolk be respectful —yet regenerative—in its pristine location.

The curving, layered façade is an expression of the coast. Color tones are drawn from sand and ocean, anchoring the building in its Queensland location.

Each apartment design subtly recedes to showcase the water views. Boundaries are blurred to feel like you are fully immersed in the landscape beyond.

Norfolk drew inspiration from the Norfolk pine's pinecone, which starts off closed to protect its seeds, and then opens when the weather and settings are optimum. In the same way, Norfolk's adaptable architecture suits the changing climate and evolving coastal environment.

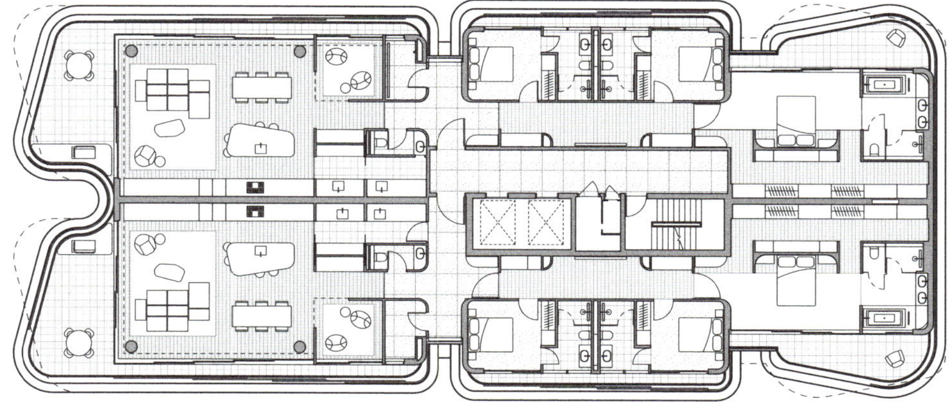

The floorplan is designed to maximize water views from every room. Recesses along the building's length break up the mass to allow natural light and ventilation throughout.

Trinity Point

2020–36

Awarded Approval

Lake Macquarie NSW, Australia Awabakal Land

Site area 36,500 m²
Floor area 42,675 m²

Six buildings with curving green roofs mark this point of land. Intended to house a luxury hotel, quality hospitality venues, and apartments, this project was designed "with a focus on providing public access to the site and increasing the landscaped foreshore." Further, according to Koichi Takada: "The natural textures and organic lines of Trinity Point aim to be more connected with landscape than built form."

The city of Lake Macquarie is located 150 kilometers north of Sydney and is named after Australia's largest coastal lagoon. Connected to the Tasman Sea, the lake covers an area of 110 square kilometers. Its shores were long inhabited by the Aboriginal Awabakal people. Used for recreational boating and water skiing, the southern edge of the lake has been designated as an Important Bird Area and is the location of the 68-hectare Pulbah Island Nature Reserve. Near the city of Newcastle, Lake Macquarie has a population of about 215,000 people. Takada's design for the Trinity Point development takes in this unusual combination of a pristine natural setting near population centers, with its forms inspired by the nearby Watagan Mountains. The client for this project already operates a restaurant nearby called 8 at Trinity, a restaurant currently operating with 350 seats until the completion of the main Trinity Point development. According to the client, the complex is to include "a luxury 200-room hotel, two 300-seat restaurants (one of which will be a newly designed 8 at Trinity), a function and business center, a wellness and day spa, multiple bars, a pool, and 218 waterfront apartments, along with the already established Trinity Point Marina which will expand to 188 berths." Takada states: "We consciously designed Trinity Point to be simultaneously iconic and understated, two seemingly incompatible concepts. The form is engaging and leaves a lasting impression, while in the landscape the curved buildings respond to the height of the foreshore tree canopy."

The project is respectful, both of the environment and local heritage. The design includes green roofs that insulate interiors and increase biodiversity, along with solar panels, rainwater capture, and a modular construction system that allows for the reduction of use of resources and waste. Second, and no less important, the Awabakal people provided "cultural training" to Takada's design team. As the architects say: "The Awabakal people did not simply live on the lake, they lived *with* the lake as part of a spiritual and cultural connection to the land and waters." It is this understanding that informed the architectural design. The connection of visitors to the site is strengthened by a master plan that gives priority to pedestrians, connecting to existing pathways so that the public will feel welcomed to the site. The subtle ways in which Koichi Takada creates a link between the site, its history, and the overall positive impact of sustainable building and design point toward new architecture that is in much closer harmony with the past and future than contemporary designs have normally been. This is no small accomplishment.

Trinity Point drew inspiration from the neighboring Watagan Mountains and the ripples of Lake Macquarie's shoreline. The Awabakal people, the traditional custodians of the land, did not simply live on the land, they lived *with* the lake and mountains, deeply connected culturally and spiritually to their environment.

The design takes a respectful approach to the history of Australia's First Nations people, including elements inspired by important local tools and materials, such as shell middens, baskets, and fish traps.

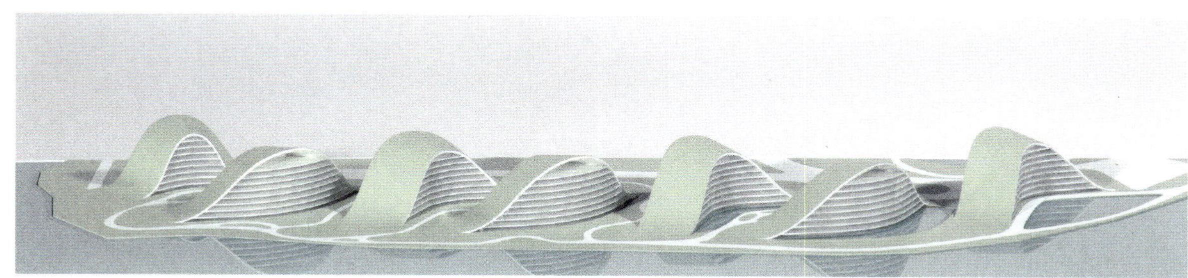

The development at Trinity Point will deliver a sensitive, mixed-use complex that increases the landscaped foreshore for public and First Nations access to the lake for "Connection to Country." A series of "rolling hills," with a gradual rise in height, provides a gentle transition to minimize the impact on the region's landscape.

Mamsha Palm

2023–28

Awarded Approval

Saadiyat Island
Abu Dhabi, UAE

Site area 2,900 m²
Floor area 11,308 m²

Saadiyat Island close to the city of Abu Dhabi is, of course, one of the most dynamic development areas of the region. It is the location of the Louvre Abu Dhabi (Jean Nouvel, 2017), the Guggenheim Abu Dhabi (Frank O. Gehry, 2025), and of the Zayed National Museum (Norman Foster, 2025). Koichi Takada joins this prestigious group in the Saadiyat Cultural District with his Mamsha Palm, a six-story, 44-unit apartment building. These residences have one to three bedrooms with floor areas ranging between 84 and 259 square meters (including balconies). The so-called "sky villas" at the upper levels have four bedrooms and floor areas of 635 to 837 square meters. Views from the top of the building include the Louvre and Guggenheim Abu Dhabi, but also the waters of the Arabian Gulf. Takada explains: "The architecture is inspired by nature, featuring flowing curves that evoke the protection of palm trees in the desert landscape. We drew aesthetic and functional cues from the tranquility of Japanese Zen lifestyle." More specifically, the architect contrasts the dynamic, even futuristic, development of Abu Dhabi with a more tranquil spirit. He says: "I also strive to create the space of what we call in Japan *iyashi*, a sense of retreat through our design, an escape from demanding urban lifestyles; similar to the effect nature has on lifting your energy and recharging your mind. Luxury to me is allowing space to breathe; an environment that allows the concept of time to disappear." The Japanese word *iyashi* is translated by a series of words in English such as healing, soothing, therapy, comfort, and solace. Amenities in the building include a rooftop wellness area, state-of-the-art gym, yoga studio, a swimming pool with panoramic views of the Arabian (Persian) Gulf, as well as a Zen garden lobby and Japanese-inspired tearoom and a children's play area.

Set in a more solid podium, the tree-like upper part of the building contains the apartments, with "palm-inspired" balconies that of course serve to shade the building, but are also evocative, according to the architect, of Abu Dhabi's Al Ain Oasis, 155 kilometers east of Abu Dhabi city. As he clearly states: "We drew aesthetic and functional cues from the Al Ain Oasis." The oasis is known for its 146,000 date palms and *falaj* irrigation systems that use underground tunnels to transport water over long distances. Promotion for the project by the client and developer Aldar has included references to other Takada projects that evoke trees, such as Upper House in Brisbane, with its "twisting roots" that rise 33 stories, and the "architectural forest" of the Solar Trees Marketplace in Shanghai.

Mamsha Palm is an “urban oasis” inspired by the protective shelter of palm trees in the desert. The form mimics the date palm, which is a symbol of life and sustenance in the arid environment, recreating the interplay of light and shadow.

"Mamsha Palm offered a rare chance to craft a vision deeply rooted in place and culture," says Koichi Takada. The mixed-use, multi-residential project on Saadiyat Island is bound by a triangulated site, alongside the pristine beach and in close proximity to a high concentration of global cultural institutions.

1 Guggenheim, Abu Dhabi
Gehry Partners, LLP
2 Louvre, Abu Dhabi
Ateliers Jean Nouvel
3 Natural History Museum
Mecanoo
4 Mamsha Palm
Koichi Takada Architects
5 Zayed National Museum
Foster + Partners
6 Abrahamic Family House
Adjaye Associates
7 teamLab Phenomena, Abu Dhabi
teamLab
8 Bassam Freiha Art Foundation
Rasha Gebran, ADD Consultants
9 Manarat Al Saadiyat
10 UAE Pavilion and Berklee
Abu Dhabi
Foster + Partners

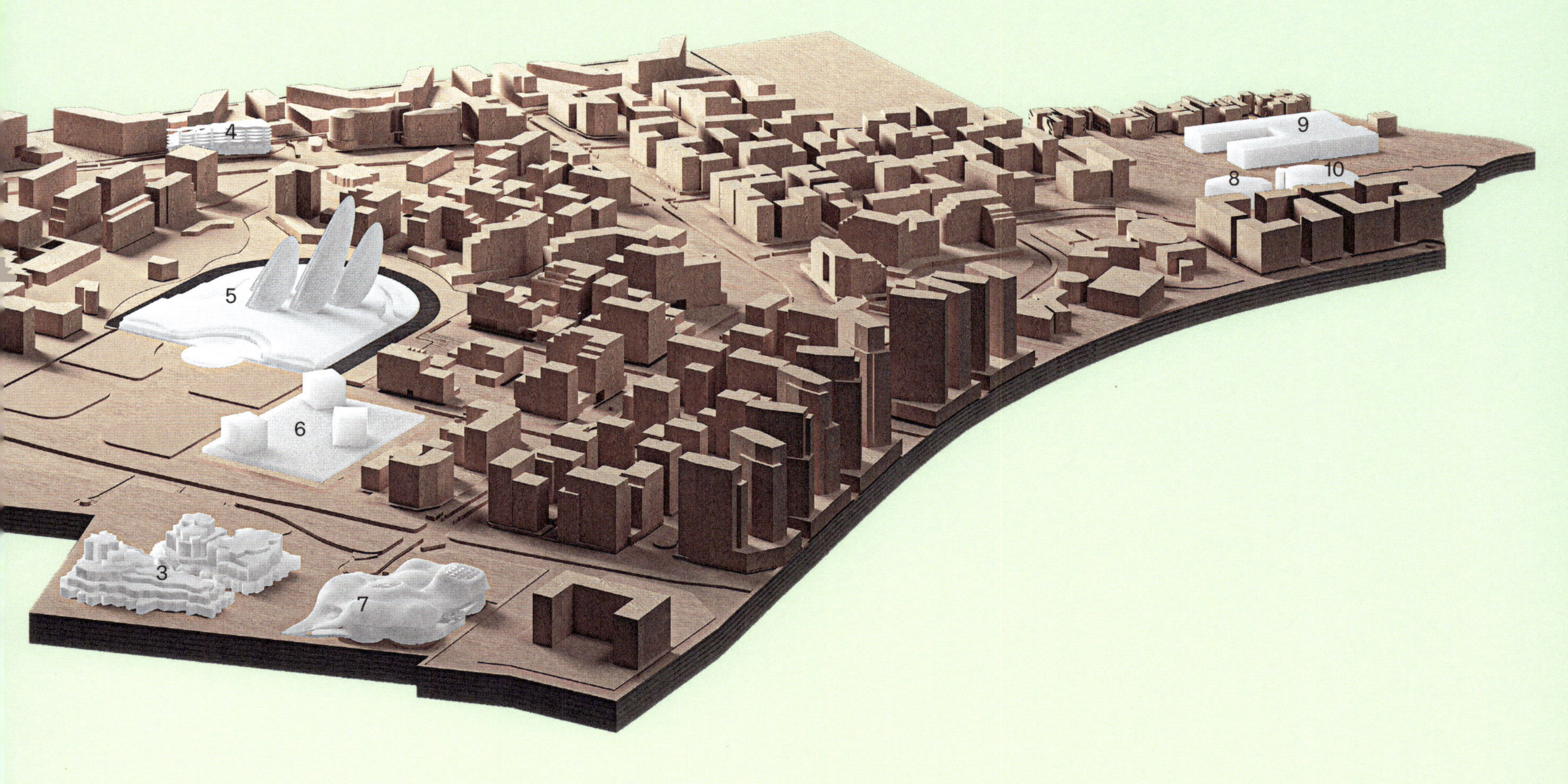

Saadiyat Island's Cultural District (Abu Dhabi, UAE) is designed to house a high concentration of iconic art, culture, and educational institutions.

Afterword

Koichi Takada

When studying architecture in New York City, Koichi Takada found refuge in the city's Central Park, "the green lung of Manhattan." This man-made greenspace triggered the questioning that informs Takada's work: "Why can't architecture be more like Central Park?" Designed by humans, perfected by nature.

In 2002, I won first prize in an international architectural design competition judged by a panel chaired by Toyo Ito, alongside esteemed Japanese architects Riken Yamamoto, Itsuko Hasegawa, and Kengo Kuma.

However, at the grand ceremony in Tokyo, the judges openly questioned whether I should have won. Puzzled, I asked why. They explained that they had struggled to see any "architecture" in my nature-inspired submission, which proposed a green roofscape to mitigate Tokyo's heat-island effect.

Determined to defend my "green" scheme, I immediately sought out Toyo Ito to discuss it with him directly. Unfortunately, he was absent, on his way to the Venice Biennale to accept the Golden Lion award for Lifetime Achievement.

Five years passed before I finally met Toyo Ito in person. After he gave a lecture in Sydney, I seized the opportunity to approach him, eager to discuss my controversial scheme. I was flattered to hear he remembered my competition entry. In discussion of my "non-architectural" approach, I mentioned Dutch practice OMA's proposal for the 1982 Parc de la Villette competition. I argued that had Rem Koolhaas won instead of Bernard Tschumi the project might have evolved differently. Perhaps today, a Koolhaas-designed Parc de la Villette would have been more aligned with contemporary principles of landscape urbanism; a perpetual work in progress, Koolhaas's Parc de la Villette would have grown and flourished as Europe's answer to the man-made New York Central Park. And today, his vision could have reached a more complete state and, more importantly, been more relevant to contemporary discourse around sustainability.

In 2017, almost a decade into running my own practice, I had the pleasure of collaborating with Kengo Kuma on an architectural competition with the City of Sydney. It was a rare opportunity to rekindle the line of questioning that had begun with my 2002 Tokyo roofscape scheme.

As we worked together, I was fascinated by how Kuma and his practice sought to blur, soften, or even "erase" architecture through nature—an approach that deeply resonated with my own philosophy. I came to a profound realization: the act of questioning itself is more powerful than any answer. In fact, our architectural collaboration for the City of Sydney—a landscape tower of "stacked forests"—defied conventional architectural expression, just as I had done 15 years earlier. While unorthodox, it was ultimately appreciated and, together, Kuma and I won the competition.

Even after devastating events like Australia's 2020 Black Summer bushfires, nature shows a remarkable ability to regenerate. Koichi Takada asserts that nature can be a powerful and profound teacher, with more than three billion years of life on planet Earth to tap into—if we take the time to listen.

Looking back on my journey of nearly three decades of practicing architecture, I realize that much of my work responds to the very questions raised during that competition in Tokyo in 2002. The ceremony became a turning point for me—one where my validation (or very nearly invalidation) as a young architect ignited a deeper drive—my *ikigai*—to pursue my own answers. The skepticism of those esteemed judges shaped my discourse, inspired me to explore my practice more deeply, and pushed me to evolve my approach to architecture.

To me, naturalizing architecture must be driven by the desire to shape a greener future. We are not there yet, but, through practice, we continue to find more natural approaches. I hope to see a day when competitions are not driven by the desire to build the tallest or most iconic structure but, rather, are motivated by a deeper commitment to sustainability and the greenest possible future.

Selected works

Cave (2009)
Restaurant
Sydney, Australia

Tree (2010)
Restaurant
Sydney, Australia

Ippudo (2012)
Restaurant
Sydney, Australia

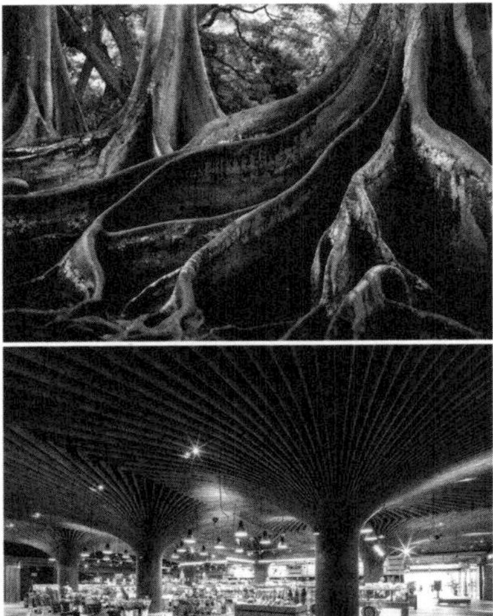

East Village (2012–15)
Retail
Sydney, Australia

One Central Park East (2012–13)
Interiors
Sydney, Australia

Skye (2012–16)
Multi-residential
Sydney, Australia

Arc (2013–18)
Mixed-use
Sydney, Australia

Infinity (2013–20)
Mixed-use
Sydney, Australia

883–889 Collins (2014–18)
Mixed-use
Melbourne, Australia

Sky Trees (2017–)
Mixed-use
Los Angeles, USA

The Mastery (2017–29)
Multi-residential
Sydney, Australia

Tree Apartment (2016–19)
Multi-residential
Sydney, Australia

Waterfront Retreat (2014–17)
Residential
Sydney, Australia

Bower (2016–19)
Multi-residential
Sydney, Australia

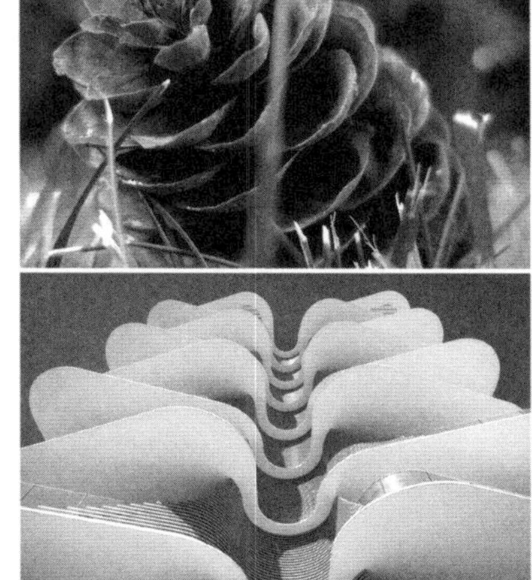
Norfolk (2019–21)
Multi-residential
Gold Coast, Australia

Burly (2022–27)
Multi-residential
Gold Coast, Australia

Waterfall (2016–29)
Multi-residential
Brisbane, Australia

Upper House (2018–23)
Multi-residential
Brisbane, Australia

Urban Forest (2020–30)
Multi-residential
Brisbane, Australia

Mooloolaba Hotel (2020–28)
Hotel
Sunshine Coast, Australia

Jiwan (2013–19)
Restaurant
Doha, Qatar

Cafe 875 (2013–19)
Restaurant
Doha, Qatar

Desert Rose (2013–19)
Restaurant
Doha, Qatar

Gift Shops NMOQ (2013–19)
Retail
Doha, Qatar

Selected works

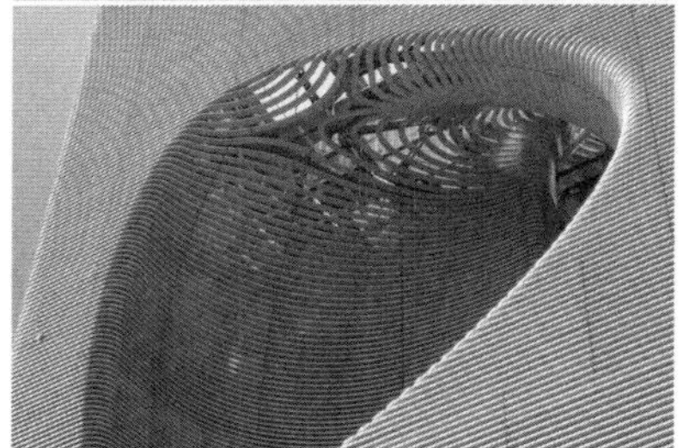

Timber Studio (2017–21)
Commercial
Tokyo, Japan

Palm Frond Retreat (2016–22)
Residential
Sydney, Australia

Yugen (2020–24)
Multi-residential
Sydney, Australia

Paperbark (2019)
Hospitality
Melbourne, Australia

Landmark by Lexus (2022–24)
Pavilion
Melbourne, Australia

Swan Suites (2019–26)
Hotel
Sydney, Australia

Cove (2019–24)
Residential
Sydney, Australia

Woolworths (2021–28)
Retail/Mixed-use
Sydney, Australia

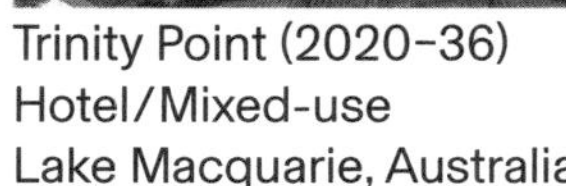

Trinity Point (2020–36)
Hotel/Mixed-use
Lake Macquarie, Australia

Chifley South (2022)
Commercial
Sydney, Australia

Sky Gardens (2023–30)
Mixed-use
Brisbane, Australia

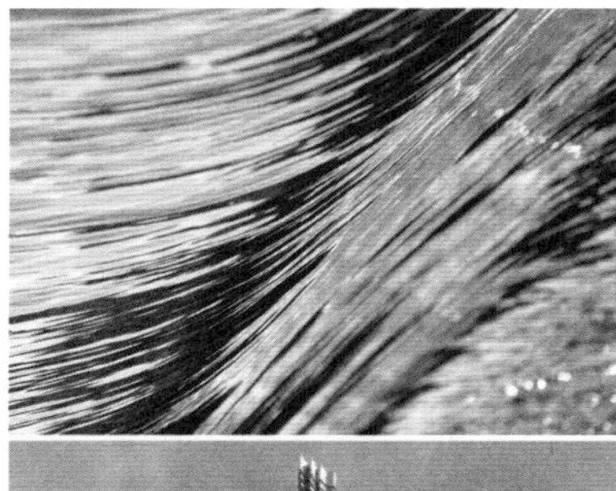

Cascade (2020–23)
Multi-residential
Chengdu, China

Sunflower House (2020)
Residential
Le Marche, Italy

Solar Trees Marketplace (2020–23)
Commercial
Shanghai, China

One Tian An Place Sports Center (2020–26)
Public buildings
Shanghai, China

Confidential (2023–30)
Retail
China

Heng Mu (2022–28)
Multi-residential
New Taipei City, Taiwan

Akasaka (2021–28)
Multi-residential
Tokyo, Japan

Thalassa (2023–27)
Residential
Palm Jumeirah, UAE

Balancing Rock (2024)
Mixed-use concept
Texas, USA

Confidential (2022–26)
Retail/Cultural
KSA

Fahid Beach Residences (2023–28)
Multi-residential
Al Fahid, Abu Dhabi, UAE

Mamsha Palm (2023–28)
Multi-residential
Saadiyat Island, Abu Dhabi, UAE

Confidential (2024)
Cultural
Morocco

Acknowledgments

I would like to extend my gratitude to the global team who brought this publication to life. Philip Jodidio (Lausanne, Switzerland) for his continued support and expertise. To Rizzoli for another opportunity to publish our "next chapter" with them. Catherine Bonifassi and the Rizzoli team (Paris, France), thank you for your direction, diligence, and patience. Thank you also to Béatrice Grenier (Paris, France) for her interrogation into the intersection of nature and architecture and to Elisa Scarton (Melbourne, Australia) for her counsel and contribution. Julien Notter (Lausanne, Switzerland), your graphic expertise is greatly appreciated. And to Alaana Cobon (Sydney, Australia), whose dedication, attention to detail, and tireless efforts were fundamental in shaping and realizing this publication. We will never forget this journey.

I am especially grateful to my long-standing directors: Georgia Wilson, who has been by my side almost since the beginning, and Terry Brabazon, whose steady guidance and knowledge, until his retirement in 2023, I am thankful for. The past 18 years have brought many challenges and opportunities, and it is with thanks to the dedication and strength of our executive team that we have grown so much together: Fabiola Cabral Monasterio, Richard Storey, Yoshi Uchiyama, Alan Zhang, Rafe Wilson, Ethan Zhang, Karen Davies, and Carolina Caponi. And to our talented staff who have contributed to each project over the years, thank you.

Further, I am grateful for the partnerships we have formed with all our clients and for the opportunities they have provided—we are honored to work with many of them time and time again: Tian An China; Aldar Properties; Bloomberg Green; Tim Forrester and the team at Aria Property Group; David Calvisi of Forme; Keith Johnson and Natalie Habib of Johnson Property Group; James Kaias; Simon White of Finegrain; John Pappas at Lexus Australia and Bruce Keebaugh of The Big Group; Icon Oceania; Aspire Development; Charter Hall; Ann Louise Donohue and David Snashall; and Vicki and Joe Mazza.

And of course, I could not do it all without Carolina by my side. You continue to spark the inspiration that shapes not just this work, but the way I see the world. I would like to dedicate this publication to Arisa, Ryu Francesco, and Alexander Issey—may they find peace and inspiration in nature, and remain curious about the world.

Koichi Takada Architects since 2008

Aaron Tregent, Abraham Fung, Adam Grasso, Adele Troger, Ady Chen, Aine Dowling, Alaana Cobon, Alan Zhang, Alejandro Pascuas, Ales Javurek, Alex (Zhenyu) Liu, Alex Rosique, Alexander Lau, Alexander Lee, Alexander Mitrevski, Alexandra Gurman, Alexzandra Issa, Alfonso Nogueira Calle, Ali Makari, Alyona Malyuk, Alyssa Saltzgaber, Amanda Tam, Ana Baez Rivero, Ana Calpanova, Andrew (Busheng) Wang, Andrew Chung, Andrew Van Zanten, Angela Garcia, Arnaud Paquier, Ashleigh Hughes, Ashley Patten, Ashley Wong, Athena Newman-Andrews, Austin Tang, Azin Shameli, Bartosz Kolodziejczuk, Beatriz Fernandez Sanchez, Ben Wright, Bianca Ezrock, Bolin Yin, Borja Pedrosa Perez, Brandon Heng Tze Ming, Bryan Wong, Bryna Hearmon, Cara Cecilio, Carmen Montejo, Carolina Caponi, Casey Woodley, Cat Crescini, Cecilia Huang, Chanelle Stark, Chiara Paolini, Chih Yun (Belle) Lee, Chiharu Ogita, Chinatsu Mitchell, Chris Isedale, Christina Sun, Clara Joly d'Aussy, Connie Yan, Cory Hartono, Crystalynn Arya, Damian Pestrin, Daniel Covarrubias, Daniel (Geun Mo) Kim, Daniel Wen, David Vernon Cardew Wilson, Denise McMaster, Dmitry Troyanovsky, Dongwoo Lee, Dookee Chung, Dorian Brennan, Elisa Scarton, Elise Vanden Dool, Ellen Lin, Emilia Grujic, Emma Cohen, Eric Lee, Eric Nakajima, Ernest (Chi Leung) Sun, Ethan (Yi Yang) Zhang, Etienne Prost, Fabiola Cabral Monasterio, Faris (Ahmad bin Ahmad) Zulfaa, Fei Halim, Felix (Hung-Wen) Tseng, Francesca d'Errico, Francis Crisp, Ganesh Hingnekar, Gema Edo Vinaras, Georgia McGowan, Georgia Wilson, Gerald Lau, Giacomo Di Bartolomeo, Giancarlo Gastaldin, Giorgia Aurigo, Grand Cheung, Gregory Fernandes, Hamed Hassani, Han Sangbeom, Hannah Ko, Harriet Powell, Hiroki Fujino, Ignacio Tello Benito, Iliea Eshow, Isabelle Reynolds, Istvan Tar, Ivan (Rui Jie) Tan, James Perry, Jana Somasundaram, Jaris Briongos Auzmendi, Jassinta Fong, Javier Saiz Merino, Jay Di, Jency Issac, Jenna Knights, Jessica Ball, Jessica Gottlieb, Jinyi Xu, Joan Lees, John Scallon, John Sham, Johnathan Nemedez, Joseph Vozzo, Joshua Downie, Jozsef Berki, Julie Hong Lien, Kai (Kai-Ting) Yang, Kai Ming Wong, Kaitlyn Sun, Kara Gurney, Karen Davies, Karolina Wlodarczyk, Kasol (Xin) Liu, Kathryn Humphreys, Katrina Passer, Ke Dai, Keira Mendoza-Kehlet, Keira Yang Zhang, Kevin Kang, Khanh Nguyen, Kris Kil, Kylie Haofei Pan, Larsa Yonan, Laura Limberger, Lia Tsatsoulis, Lisa Cohen, Lorenzo Paolieri, Luisa Moran, Luka Owens, Luke Amit Egbert Pinto, Madeleine Stewart, Madison Wright, Maha Saad, Mahsa Karkhaneh, Marcella Khusworo, Marcellino Sain, Margaret Lee, Marina Lazareva, Marina Savochkina, Marino Kubo, Marta Alfaro Azcarraga, Masa Sado, Matthew Gold, Mattias Dorph, Megan Albury, Mel Pimolsook, Melika Aljukic, Michael Juda, Michael Obrien, Michiru Cohen, Mingzhu Zhang, Minh Le, Miriam Pinkney, Mori (Jiajun) Li, Nancy Fernando, Natalia Zapata Aldana, Nermine Zahran, Nicola Sherbon, Nicole Milne, Nicole Reynolds, Nicole Vella, Nikki Greenberg, Noel Roche, Noel Samyia, Olena Maliuk, Owen Olthof, Paige Gervaise, Paolo Stracchi, Pascale Roberts, Patrick Girdler, Patrick Li, Paula Ito, Peter Brown, Prajal Rai, Priscilla Lynarko, Pu (Paul) Peng, Rachel Finkelstein, Rafael Jurado Giner, Rafael Torrelo, Rafe Wilson, Reem Mosleh, Regina Koropachinskaya, Rei Sakurai, Reichelle Carson, Reiko Iwamoto, Richard Storey, Rig (Lijing) Yu, Robert Chen, Rohan Gu, Roland Song, Ruzica Maric, Ryan Cotterill, Sahar Deljoo, Samuel Taylor, Sandra Pamplona Gascon, Sandy (Hui) Liu, Sara Fard, Sarah Shand, Scott Beer, Sean Bryen, Sean Wong, Seungsoo Lee, Shawn Li, Shellie Jackson, Shi Chen, Simon (Yiu Hang) Lee, Sisi Yao, Sneha Nedungadi, Sran Akahane Bryen, Stephen Rofail, Suba (Subashini) Ganandran, Sue (Suyeon) Mun, Takeru Sato, Tania Coneliano, Tarun Reddy, Taylor Heywood, Teresa Cruces Cuadra, Terry Brabazon, Thida Sachathep, Thomas (Tong) Huang, Tiffany Chang, Timothy Schrieber, Timothy Truong, Tommy Sutrisno, Tracy Meyer, Vernon Cheung, Victor Xian-Hao Li, Violet Tran, Vivien (Ming Yuet) Au, Vivienne Hinschen, Wen Han Fu, Wen Xin Li, Will Choi, William Page, Wing Ning (Winnie) Sheung, Xinyi (Ryan) Wang, Yarden Lavy, Yen Nhien Nguyen, Yoshi Uchiyama, Young Lee, Zhen Dai, Zigi (Zicci) Zhou, Zuzanna Robutka.

Koichi Takada Architects
Naturalizing Architecture

First published in the United States
of America in 2025 by
Rizzoli International Publications, Inc.
49 West 27th Street
New York, NY 10001
www.rizzoliusa.com

Text Philip Jodidio
Foreword Béatrice Grenier
Afterword Koichi Takada

Publisher Charles Miers
Editorial Director Catherine Bonifassi
Production Director Maria Pia Gramaglia
Managing Editor Lynn Scrabis

Design Notter+Vigne

Editorial Coordination CASSI EDITION
Vanessa Blondel, Cyriane Flamant,
Harriet Graham

ISBN 978-0-8478-7422-4
Library of Congress Control Number 2025934149

Printed in Italy
2025 2026 2027 2028 / 10 9 8 7 6 5 4 3 2 1

The authorized representative in the EU for product safety and compliance is Mondadori Libri S.p.A., via Gian Battista Vico 42, Milan, Italy, 20123
www.mondadori.it

Visit us online
Instagram.com/RizzoliBooks
Facebook.com/RizzoliNewYork
Youtube.com/user/RizzoliNY

Image and Project Credits

Cover Binyan. P. 6: Koichi Takada Architects. P. 8: Eiichi Kano. P. 9: Tupungato - stock.adobe.com. PP. 10–11: Konstantin Shishkin - stock.adobe.com. P. 12: Nic Walker. P. 14: top, Salty|snow Photography/ Wirestock Creators - stock.adobe.com; bottom, Gerald Zaffuts - stock.adobe.com. P. 16: top, iStock/shilh; bottom and right, Inplace Visual. P. 18: left, iStock/zodebala; right, Ivolve Studios. P. 19: Koichi Takada Architects. P. 20: Alamy/Kitawaki Noboru. P. 21: Brick Visual. P. 22: Courtesy Aria Property Group. P. 23: Scott Burrows, Architectural Photographer. P. 25: dougandwolf.com. P. 26: Tom Ferguson. P. 27: Inplace Visual. PP. 28–29: iStock/Natsunokujira.
Timber Studio PP. 31, 33–44: Daici Ano; p. 32: lotusjeremy - stock.adobe.com.
Solar Trees Marketplace PP. 49, 56–57: Eiichi Kano; p. 48: lotusjeremy - stock.adobe.com; pp. 47, 50–51, 52, 53, 54–55, 58–59: ZY Architectural Photography.
Upper House PP. 63, 65–67, 72, 74–75, 80–81: Scott Burrows, Architectural Photographer; pp. 68, 69, 73, 80–81: Tom Ferguson; pp. 70, 71, 76–77, 78–79, 80–81: Mark Nilon; p. 64: blickwinkel/ Alamy Stock Photo.
Urban Forest PP. 83, 85–99: Binyan; p. 84: Getty/ Ippei Naoi.
Sunflower House PP. 101, 103–104: dougandwolf.com; p. 102: iStock/Laura Noll.
Chifley South PP. 107, 109–116: Play-Time; p. 108: iStock/chinaface.
Sky Gardens PP. 119, 121–125: PLOTS Studio; p. 120: pexels/Sonny Sixteen.
Landmark by Lexus PP. 127, 129–132: Sharyn Cairns; p. 128: iStock/Paul Hobson.
Cove PP. 135, 137–147: Tom Ferguson; p. 136: hendrik-martin- stock.adobe.com.
Tree Apartment PP. 149, 151–153, 155–156, 158: Bryn Donkersloot; pp. 154, 157, 159, 160: Tom Ferguson; p. 150: iStock-1349073227.
Yugen P. 163: The Two Artisans; 165–167, 174: Simon Whitbread; pp. 168–173: Martin Siegner; p. 164: iStock/Vu Viet Dung;
Palm Frond Retreat PP. 177, 179–191: Tom Ferguson; p. 178: Koichi Takada Architects.
Norfolk PP. 193, 196, 198–201, 209 top left: Scott Burrows, Architectural Photographer; pp. 195, 202, 204–205: Tom Ferguson; p. 194: HN Works - stock.adobe.com; pp. 197, 203: Paul Bamford; pp. 206–207, 209 top right: Cieran Murphy; p. 209: Koichi Takada Architects.
Trinity Point PP. 211, 213–218: FloodSlicer; p. 212: iStock/Adam88xx.
Mamsha Palm P. 221: dougandwolf.com; p. 222: iStock/Rob Jones; pp. 223–225: Bucharest Studio.
PP. 228–229: Jem Chen. P. 230: Craig Fruchtman. P. 230: The Mastery Render - dougandwolf.com. P. 232: iStock/Philip Thurston. P. 233: naturalearth2 - stock.adobe.com.

Collaborators

Shimizu Corporation (Timber Studio); LDI: Shanghai Tianhua Architecture Planning & Engineering Ltd and Shanghai Strait Land Real Estate Co., Ltd (Solar Trees Marketplace); Minicon and Theca Timber (Upper House); SFN Build Pty Ltd (Cove); Construction Profile (Tree Apartment); Reform Projects (Yugen); Builder Artechne and Interiors by Justine Hugh-Jones (Palm Frond Retreat); Interiors by MIM Design, Hutchinson Builders and documentation services by Plus Architects (Norfolk).